THE WOODSTOCK BRANCH

BY

STANLEY C. JENKINS MA

WILD SWAN PUBLICATIONS LTD.

TRAFFIC DEALT WITH AT STATIONS

Station.	Year.	Staff. Supervisory and Wages (all Grades).	Staff. Paybill Expenses.	Total Receipts.	Passenger Train Traffic. Tickets issued.	Season Tickets.	Receipts. Passengers (including Season Tickets, etc.)	Receipts. Parcels.	Receipts. Miscellaneous.	Receipts. Total.	Goods Train Traffic. Forwarded. Coal and Coke "Charged."	Forwarded. Other Minerals.	Forwarded. General Merchandise.	Received. Coal and Coke "Charged."	Received. Other Minerals.	Received. General Merchandise.	Coal and Coke "Not Charged" (Forwarded and Received).	Total Goods Tonnage.	Total Receipts (excluding "Not Charged" Coal and Coke).	Livestock (Forwarded and Received).	Total Carted Tonnage (Included in Total Goods Tonnage).
		No.	£	£	No.	No.	£	£	£	£	Tons	Tons.	Tons.	Tons.	Tons.	Tons.	Tons.	Tons.	£	Wagons.	Tons.
Blenheim Branch.																					
Shipton-on-Cherwell Halt.				Opened	April, 1929.																
Blenheim and Woodstock. (‡)	1903	*	*	5,386	17,436	*	1,576	668	240	2,484		46	744	427	1,695	1,877	3,715	8,504	2,902	128	1,084
	1913	5	308	5,610	17,168	*	1,475	559	222	2,256		89	1,180	753	1,746	2,295	2,866	8,929	3,354	242	1,000
	1923	7	897	9,376	19,117	236	2,529	705	144	3,378	14	23	2,482	420	2,017	2,061	4,433	11,450	5,998	85	935
	1924	7	1,081	8,215	17,265	253	2,441	631	182	3,254	15	16	1,707	439	1,240	2,310	4,800	10,527	4,961	85	908
	1925	7	1,095	8,471	17,253	218	2,246	662	285	3,193		164	1,398	355	2,945	2,204	4,812	11,878	5,278	96	870
	1926	6	900	9,080	15,200	239	1,857	639	334	2,830	38	448	1,896	493	3,912	1,999	2,867	11,653	6,250	107	896
	1927	6	895	8,914	16,589	292	1,910	754	370	3,034		804	1,741	761	1,573	2,115	5,053	12,047	5,880	131	950
	1928	6	801	7,654	15,752	238	1,884	687	259	2,830	47	262	1,377	614	1,371	2,006	4,504	10,181	4,824	137	942
	1929	6	802	6,875	15,985	153	1,520	655	207	2,382	18	94	909	825	2,917	1,586	5,199	11,548	4,493	112	800
	1930	5	655	6,627	15,566	91	1,206	613	169	1,988	18	187	1,284	751	2,160	1,427	4,925	10,752	4,639	67	769
	1931	5	676	5,758	13,003	54	985	526	195	1,706	16	123	809	597	3,358	1,225	5,008	11,136	4,052	25	767
	1932	5	674	5,257	15,023	38	1,196	631	158	1,985	14	165	918	847	839	963	4,312	8,058	3,272	30	761
	1933	4	594	4,817	23,295	22	1,295	674	64	2,033		67	620	540	1,077	930	4,069	7,303	2,784	29	728
Kidlington .. (§)	1903	9	*	3,010	15,480	*	816	168	128	1,112	—	94	1,951	53	12	1,284	1,495	4,889	1,808	47	227
	1913	10	507	2,921	16,537	*	788	113	239	1,140	8	8	1,476	33	1,326	861	1,116	4,828	1,781	119	277
	1923	10	1,438	4,461	13,423	88	1,034	242	373	1,649	8	—	1,311	46	286	1,369	914	3,934	2,812	104	853
	1924	10	1,431	7,153	9,737	63	823	285	434	1,542	8	10	2,371	29	328	1,516	835	5,097	5,611	664	684
	1925	11	1,563	8,508	7,928	60	670	372	707	1,749	—	4	2,755	47	374	1,759	1,155	6,094	6,759	854	976
	1926	11	1,430	6,728	6,173	52	541	322	872	1,735	11	125	2,094	48	1,403	1,363	740	5,784	4,993	470	442
	1927	10	1,350	6,324	6,591	35	496	216	499	1,211	5	913	1,181	137	4,305	1,162	1,625	9,328	5,113	279	315
	1928	10	1,287	5,417	6,958	83	512	153	357	1,022	—	3,001	859	85	4,251	1,530	1,564	11,290	4,395	147	303
	1929	10	1,335	4,969	6,533	27	442	112	281	835	—	79	434	108	6,277	1,459	1,787	10,144	4,134	88	199
	1930	10	1,289	3,592	6,656	30	438	127	324	889	—	26	563	113	2,841	1,052	1,211	5,806	2,703	112	145
	1931	10	1,295	2,945	6,490	39	440	151	256	847	—	33	505	232	1,002	971	1,510	4,253	2,098	113	174
	1932	10	1,290	3,087	6,300	10	393	210	57	660	5	—	285	277	3,070	930	1,541	6,108	2,427	100	372
	1933	10	1,284	2,593	6,880	10	466	229	73	768	—	1	264	245	1,972	830	1,402	4,714	1,825	88	525

* Not available.

§ Controls Blenheim and Woodstock.

Rear cover: '1076' class 0–6–0PT No. 1294 with a Woodstock Branch train in February 1931. *(Dr. I. C. Allen)*

ACKNOWLEDGEMENTS

Thanks are due to the following individuals or organisations who have contributed photographs or information: Chris Turner, Lens of Sutton, Paul Karau, Jim Russell, Colin Judge, P. J. T. Reed, Mrs. R. Giraud, Miss F. Budd, C. J. Bond, David & Charles Ltd., W. A. Camwell, F. J. Agar, F. M. Butterfield, J. E. Kite, Sean Bolan, Adrian Vaughan, R. M. Casserley, John Rhodes, Malcolm Graham, R. H. G. Simpson, J. H. Moss, C. L. Turner, Miss Sian Rule, Ivel Hornbrook, Mrs. F. Winfield, Dr. G. D. Parkes, P. B. Whitehouse, Gerry Beale, R. C. Riley, R. J. Buckley and British Railways. Also the staffs of the Westgate Library, Oxford, and the University Library, Leicester, the Oxfordshire County Records Office, the Public Records Office, Kew, the City & County Museum, Woodstock, and Miss Malcolm of Witney Library.

ISBN 0 906867 51 7

Designed by Paul Karau
Printed by Netherwood Dalton & Co., Huddersfield

Published by
WILD SWAN PUBLICATIONS LTD.
1-3 Hagbourne Road, Didcot, Oxon OX11 8DP

CONTENTS

INTRODUCTION

The Great Western Railway built (or acquired) a varied assortment of attractive rural branch lines, many of which are justly famous. Inevitably, the seaside routes in Devon and Cornwall have enjoyed much attention, but not all Great Western branches served the far west; there was another group of classic country branch lines in and around the Thames Valley, and these London Division lines were every bit as interesting as their West Country counterparts. The Woodstock line, for example, was an archetypal GWR branch. Opened as recently as 1890, the line was situated on the periphery of the Oxfordshire Cotswolds, and was just 3¾ miles long — though as it ran parallel to the Oxford to Birmingham main line for well over a mile, its apparent length was nearer 2½ miles. The Woodstock branch was an essentially simple affair, small in scale and intimate in character. Sadly its life was short and the last trains had run by 1954, just 64 years after the first public working had steamed proudly into Woodstock station. Fortunately, the branch was recorded photographically throughout its brief life, and thanks to much hard work carried out by Paul Karau and others, many rare and interesting illustrations have been painstakingly assembled. It is hoped that the narrative will expand and complement the illustrative material — and perhaps throw light on aspects of the Woodstock branch that have not yet been fully explored. It is hoped that the following text and photographs will form a worthy memorial to a little railway that was born in hope, flourished for a few years, and is now gone.

Stanley C. Jenkins
Witney, Oxfordshire 1987

A Note on Punctuation & Proper Nouns

Certain legal and Parliamentary documents quoted in Chapter Two were unpunctuated, and to prevent confusion (for example, in the case of lists of nouns) a limited number of commas have been inserted; this is in a sense a case of 'tampering' with original material but it was felt that the interests of readers should come first — the overriding aim being to produce a coherent, readable narrative.

The Woodstock Railway Company called its terminus Blenheim & Woodstock, and in practice this was often shortened to *Blenheim* rather that Woodstock; 'Blenheim' and 'Woodstock' are thus interchangeable, although Blenheim is perhaps the most accurate form. Kidlington was called 'Woodstock Road' until 19th May 1890, but, confusingly, nearby Bletchington was originally called Woodstock Road; in general however, the 'Woodstock Road' referred to in chapters 1, 2 and 5 is Kidlington.

Market Street, Woodstock, looking west towards Park Street, with the Kings Arms Hotel to the right and the Town Hall visible in the left distance. This view probably dates from around 1926, by which time motor cars had become familiar sights on rural roads. *Packer Collection, Oxfordshire County Museums Services, Woodstock*

CHAPTER ONE

ORIGINS OF THE WOODSTOCK BRANCH

WOODSTOCK is a small, Cotswold stone town, situated some six miles north-west of Oxford. In ancient times, this area of Oxfordshire was part of the Forest of Wychwood, and many of the surrounding villages have Saxon names relating to trees or woodland; Woodstock itself is a corruption of 'Woodstoe' or the 'woody place'.

The Domesday Book records that Woodstock was a Royal Manor, and in medieval times the Plantagenet kings frequently stayed in the area. Henry I built a hunting lodge here in the early 12th century, enclosing part of Wychwood Forest to form a 'Park' (in which he kept a menagerie of lions, tigers and other beasts). Henry's grandson, the large, bad-tempered, red-headed and leonine Henry II, also spent much of his time at Woodstock, enlarging the hunting lodge and granting 'divers portions of . . . the demesne . . . to divers men for the purpose of building lodgings therein'. In this way, royal patronage encouraged urban growth, and it could be argued, with some justification, that Woodstock was created by Henry II. Posterity, however, has chosen to link Henry with Woodstock in a very different way, and many guide books relate how the King visited his hunting lodge 'for love of a certain woman named Rosamund'. This lady was Rosamund Clifford, the daughter of Walter de Clifford, a benefactor of nearby Godstow Nunnery.

Legend suggests that Henry visited 'Fair Rosamund' in some secret bower within the depths of Woodstock Park, until his Queen, Eleanor of Aquitaine, discovered the bower and confronted Rosamund — offering her the choice of death by dagger or poison. Sadly this picturesque tale is pure fabrication, for Henry visited his mistress quite openly at a time when the Queen was herself a virtual prisoner; Rosamund died naturally at Woodstock and was carried in state to Godstow Nunnery, where she was buried beneath the High Altar, her tomb becoming a shrine for the local peasantry! (As we shall see, Fair Rosamund was destined to have an especial association with the Woodstock branch, and for this reason her story is of some relevance to later events.)

Woodstock remained a popular royal abode throughout the Middle Ages, and the former hunting lodge was eventually transformed into a royal 'palace'; Henry III escaped assassination there in 1238, while Edward III and Queen Philippa resided in the medieval palace on several occasions, notably in 1330 when the Queen gave birth to Edward, the Black Prince. Indeed, most of the medieval kings stayed in Woodstock at various times, and this former woodland village was undoubtedly a place of some importance during the Middle Ages.

Woodstock was in decline during the Tudor period — though its royal associations continued when the future Elizabeth I was imprisoned in the old palace by her half-sister, the Catholic Mary I. In 1642 the decaying (and probably half-ruinous) medieval palace was garrisoned by Royalist forces as part of an outer rim of defences protecting the King's headquarters at Oxford. The town was surrendered to Parliament on 26th April 1646 and what was left of the royal palace was demolished in 1651 (the story of this siege inspired Sir Walter Scott to write his Civil War novel, *Woodstock*).

Woodstock remained a royal manor until 1704, in which year the property was conferred on John Churchill, the First Duke of Marlborough, as a reward for his great victory over Louis IV at the Battle of Blenheim. Henceforth Woodstock would be dominated by a landed magnate, and the interests of the town inevitably became subordinate to the wishes of those who dwelt in a massive new palace, built near the site of Henry II's old hunting lodge. Blenheim Palace itself took over twenty years to build and cost at least £300,000 — a huge sum in those days. Designed by John Vanburgh and Nicholas Hawksmoor, it eventually covered seven acres; at one time over 1,500 workmen were employed in its construction. When finally completed in 1725 the magnificent palace was not unlike Versailles — that symbol of a French monarch whose ambitions had been humbled on the field of Blenheim on 13th August 1704.

Pre-Railway Trade & Transport

Resident landlords invariably retard industrial development, and this seems to have been the case at Woodstock where glove-making, the local industry, remained based on the domestic system, with large numbers of outworkers painstakingly sewing gloves in their own cottages. On sunny days, female workers would sit at their cottage doors, busily plying their ancient craft, while the menfolk could often be seen preparing raw sheepskins by stretching and bleaching them in fields and open spaces around the town. Although these diverse operations might have been carried out more effectively in modern factories, the inhabitants of Blenheim Palace would hardly welcome the appearance of large new factories on their doorstep! On the other hand, successive Dukes did much to improve local agriculture, and the Fourth Duke of Marlborough was an enthusiastic canal promoter and a major supporter of the Oxford Canal (which ran across his land within 1½ miles of Woodstock).

Rivers were the highways of pre-industrial England, and the Thames, flowing from west to east some 4 miles south of Woodstock, enabled stone, timber and agricultural produce from the Duke's estates to be sent downstream to London. In wintertime (when water was in ample supply) adventurous barge masters somehow managed to prod, pole or haul their cumbersome vessels along many miles of barely-navigable waterway, and it is conceivable that such voyages could have been made along the rivers Cherwell or Evenlode towards Woodstock. Indeed the southern section of the Oxford Canal was in effect merely an improved River Cherwell, and, when opened to traffic in 1789/90, this new waterway utilised the riverbed for several miles. Meanwhile, the opening of the Thames & Severn Canal from the Severn to the Thames at Lechlade did much to increase the value of existing river links, and in 1789 the Fourth Duke himself opened a short connecting waterway between the Oxford Canal and the Thames at Wolvercote.

Having become something of a canal 'enthusiast', the enterprising Duke next considered a scheme involving the River Evenlode, and in 1802 the engineer Robert Milne suggested that the river might be made properly navigable from Charlbury to its confluence with the Thames at Cassington. If fully implemented this scheme would have provided useful water facilities on the western side of Blenheim Park, but, in the event, only 56 chains of waterway were ever constructed and, when opened in 1802, the canal extended no further than the Duke's corn mill at Cassington. Nevertheless, these canals enabled coal, salt and lime to reach the Blenheim estates, and their construction shows that the Churchills were not afraid to spend considerable sums of money on expensive transport schemes.

Although none of these waterways served Woodstock directly, local traders were able to use road transport in order to reach wharves at Thrupp, Eynsham or Cassington and by 18th-century standards it could be said that the town was well-endowed with transport facilities. In addition to its canal links, the town was conveniently situated on the Oxford to Stratford turnpike, and passing traffic obviously helped the local economy in many ways. Stage coaches called regularly at the Bear, the Star and the Marlborough Arms hotels, while humbler travellers might take their meals at several smaller inns and taverns. By the 1830s Woodstock had become a recognised 'coaching town' and, in the absence of large scale industry, many local people found employment as innkeepers, stablemen or servants. The development of railways, however, posed a serious threat to road transport and to Woodstock itself — for the little town was avoided by all the early railway schemes.

The Oxford & Rugby line and 'Woodstock Rd' Station

Apart from a rather premature project of the 1820s (when the pioneering Stratford & Moreton horse tramway had surveyed a possible extension running south-westward along the Evenlode valley), the first railway to approach anywhere near Woodstock was the Great Western, which was opened from Reading to Steventon on 1st June 1840. The GWR was completed throughout its length from London to Bristol on 30th June 1841, and three years later, on 12th June 1844, the company opened a 9 mile 57 chain branch from Didcot to Oxford. Plans were soon afoot to extend this line northwards, and in the early months of 1845 two related Bills were laid before Parliament. Both were for 7 ft gauge lines diverging from the existing railhead at Oxford; the 'Oxford & Rugby Railway' would run due north along the Cherwell valley to join the Midland Counties Railway at Rugby, while the 'Oxford, Worcester & Wolverhampton Railway' would strike north-west to Worcester and thence to a junction with the Grand Junction Railway at Wolverhampton.

If successful, these projected railways would tap traffic to and from Lancashire, Yorkshire and the Midlands and funnel it onto the Great Western via Oxford. Unfortunately, this ambitious scheme was presented to Parliament at a time when there was much concern in Government circles over the evils of a 'Break of Gauge', and the two Great Western Bills were subjected to careful scrutiny at the committee stage. Over 100 witnesses gave answers to 12,148 questions, and the proceedings eventually appeared in a massive official report. The Parliamentary Committee finally decided in favour of the broad gauge lines — though they added a special clause to the Oxford & Rugby Bill, obliging the GWR to provide a mixed gauge track if called upon to do so by the Board of Trade.

In spite of determined opposition from the London & Birmingham Railway, the Midland Railway, and the well-known Free Trader Richard Cobden, the Oxford, Worcester & Wolverhampton Bill was passed by the House of Commons by 247 votes to 113, and the Oxford & Rugby Bill was later passed by 79 votes to 43. Both Bills were given a third reading on 24th June, and sent up to the House of Lords. On the following day, Cobden moved a resolution proposing a Royal Commission to investigate the gauge question. This resolution was passed without opposition and the Royal Commission was set up on 9th July. Meanwhile, a Lords Committee had pronounced in favour of the two broad gauge Bills, and the Oxford, Worcester & Wolverhampton and Oxford & Rugby schemes received the Royal Assent on 4th August 1845.

The Oxford & Rugby Act empowered the GWR to construct a railway linking its Oxford branch to Rugby, a distance of 51 miles. This new line would run due north across the flat meadowlands of the Upper Thames Valley, then penetrate the oolitic limestone of the Oxfordshire Cotswolds via the Cherwell Valley. Although there would be no large bridges or other works *en route*, the serpentine nature of the River Cherwell would require many small underbridges; north of Kidlington, for example, there would be eight such structures in only four miles. Furthermore, the presence of the Oxford Canal — which ran parallel to the Cherwell and in places actually shared its route — meant that adequate headroom would have to be provided, and thus the new railway would be on embankments for much of its length.

The work was let as a single contract in the autumn of 1845, but there was delay in getting possession of the land, and construction did not begin until the summer of 1846. Unfortunately, long periods of cold and abysmally wet weather hindered the railway builders, and — perhaps more seriously — caused the harvest to fail. This in turn plunged Europe into a severe trade depression, and in 1847 work on the Oxford & Rugby line came to a standstill. A new contractor was installed in April 1848, but with most of Europe aflame with revolutions and political unrest, the prevailing economic climate remained uncongenial, and little progress was made. Finally, in the summer of 1849, the GWR decided to abandon 15½ miles of the projected route north of Fenny Compton, and to concentrate instead on the 24 mile long southern section between Oxford and Banbury. As there appeared to be no immediate prospect of any connection with narrow gauge lines, the railway was to be opened as a broad gauge line.

In April 1850 the Chairman of the GWR approached the Railway Commissioners for permission to open the Oxford & Rugby as a 7 ft gauge line. At first, the Commissioners seemed agreeable, but, under pressure from narrow gauge factions, they later tried to hold the Great Western to the provisions of the Oxford & Rugby Act. The powers of the Railway Commissioners were, however, ill-defined, and (perhaps because of this) the GWR ignored all protests and went ahead with the opening. The line was inspected by Captain Simmons, H.M. Inspector of Railways, on 27th August 1850, and the inspector reported that in his mind there was nothing affecting the safety of the public to prevent its opening as a single line. Thus, with apparent official approval, the Oxford & Rugby Railway was opened, in defiance of its Act, on Monday, 2nd September 1850.

The new railway was, as yet, little more than a rural branch line; it left the Oxford branch at 'Millstream Junction', in the Hinksey area of Oxford, and ran northwards to Banbury, a distance of 24 miles and 15 chains. Intermediate stations were provided at 'Woodstock Road', Heyford and Aynho, and the line was worked by a single engine. Civil engineering was simple, with wooden canal and river bridges that would not have been out of place in the American West; the largest bridge, over the Thames at Oxford, had three wrought iron spans, two of 32 ft and a central opening of 62 ft. Other features of the line were its standard Brunelian track and architecture; the track consisted of bridge rails laid on longitudinal timber sleepers, while the station at Banbury had a typical Brunel timber roof. Intermediate stations were provided with small rectangular station buildings which were probably constructed of wood, and ground plans of the station known as 'Woodstock Road' suggest that these stations originally resembled the standard, pre-fabricated wooden shacks that were erected all over the Great Western system during the 1850s.

Meanwhile, the shifting sands of railway politics had led to formation of the 'Birmingham & Oxford Junction Railway', which effectively extended the Oxford & Rugby route north to Birmingham and the Midlands, and in 1852 (when broad gauge trains commenced running between London, Oxford and Birmingham) the Oxford & Rugby became part of an important main line. Unfortunately, the Oxford Worcester & Wolverhampton route was thereby relegated to secondary status, and this resulted in a major row between the GWR and its former protégé. When opened throughout on 4th June 1853 the Oxford to Worcester line was a standard gauge route, openly supported by the London & North Western Railway, and in the following year OW & WR trains started running through to Euston in defiance of the GWR.

These complex developments are unlikely to have troubled either the Churchills or their Woodstock tenants — who now had main line stations conveniently situated to the east and west of their little town. The Oxford & Rugby station at 'Woodstock Road' was replaced by a new 'Woodstock Road' in 1855, and thereafter the original station became known as Kirtlington (later Bletchington). Situated some 2 miles 7 chains south of the first station, the new Woodstock Road was provided with solidly-constructed 'Brunel' style buildings and a standard broad gauge-type goods shed. Although it was 3 miles south-east of Woodstock, carriers' carts enabled townsfolk to reach their station in relative comfort, and Woodstock Road functioned successfully as a local railhead.

The OW & WR station at Handborough provided an alternative facility some three miles south west of Woodstock, and in a sense it could be argued that the inhabitants of the town were lucky to have this choice of stations and routes. Woodstock was, after all, merely a small country town with a population of only 1,300. Unlike neighbouring Witney or Chipping Norton, it had no industries of any real significance, and under the circumstances there was no *real* need for a direct rail link — other than perhaps local pride. The fact that such a rail link was eventually built is therefore something of a mystery; it is however possible to suggest several reasons why the line *might* have been built.

Woodstock & The Churchills in the 1880s

Woodstock was in a state of gradual decline throughout the 19th century. In part, this was a result of agricultural depression, but lack of industrial employment was also an important consideration; with jobs in short supply many young families simply drifted away to find work in Oxford or other large cities, and this steady migration was reflected in a declining local population. The Churchills, in contrast, were on the crest of a wave. The Seventh Duke, John Winston Spencer Churchill (1822–1883), had been an ardent reformer, dedicated to popular education, sabbath day observance and improved conditions for the labouring classes. The Seventh Duke had probably toyed with the idea of bringing a railway to his native town — hoping, however, that such a line would be built by the GWR. Indeed, late in 1882 the Duke had offered to convey, free of charge, land for a branch line between Woodstock and the Great Western main line at Woodstock Road station. The GWR directors referred the matter to their engineers, but nothing positive had been done at the time of the Seventh Duke's death in 1883. Blenheim and its estate then passed to his eldest son, George Charles Spencer Churchill (1844–1892), the Eighth Duke of Marlborough.

Although the new Duke had inherited the estate and title, he was in many ways overshadowed by his younger brother, the dashing Lord Randolph Churchill. In 1874, Lord Randolph — then only twenty-five — was elected MP for Woodstock, and this ambitious young politician spent much time at Blenheim (where his son Winston was born in November 1874). By the 1880s, Lord Randolph had emerged as leader of the so-called 'Fourth Party' — an unofficial grouping of younger Tories who hoped to present their political creed to the masses in a popular and exciting way. Like other third or fourth parties, it was sometimes difficult to see what the 'Fourth Party' stood for, but there was no doubting its grass roots popularity. Huge rallies became a feature of political life, and Lord Randolph, together with his striking American wife Jennie (1854–1921), would tour the great centres of population in a conscious and unashamed attempt to 'woo the masses'.

Politics were at that time in a state of flux. The Franchise Bill of 1884 had increased the British electorate from 3,000,000 to 5,000,000 and (at a time when Gladstone's Liberal Party was seen as a party of free-trading industrialists) the Tories began to portray themselves as champions of the *working man* as well as a party of great landowners. To further this aim a group of 'Fourth Party' MPs founded an organisation known as the Primrose League — a political society which was supposed to 'embrace all classes and all creeds except atheists and enemies of the British Empire'. Lady Randolph rapidly became a leading figure in this new organisation, while the Duchess of Marlborough was made President of the Ladies' Grand Council.

The Fourth Party and the Primrose League were both intimately connected with Blenheim, and, although the borough of Woodstock was disfranchised in 1885, Lord Randolph — a superb orator with an instinctive understanding of the masses — must have realised that his ancestral home would provide a splendid, theatrical setting for speeches and political rallies. However, as Lady Randolph later recalled, 'the distances to cover were great, and motors were not in existence'. Clearly, if Blenheim Palace could be reached by rail this transport problem would be overcome and the party faithful could reach Woodstock in large numbers. It is conceivable that Randolph was able to persuade his brother that a rail link would be a good idea, and here is one possible motive for the building of a branch line to Woodstock.

A second, and perhaps more obvious, motive may have been a simple desire on the part of the Eighth Duke to improve the lot of his tenants. The people of Woodstock had long desired a railway of their own, and, following the example set by his canal-building ancestor, the Duke may have felt that it was a *duty* to provide something for 'his' people. There had moreover been a feeling that Woodstock had been neglected by the Seventh Duke, who had an Anglo-Irish wife and had served as Lord Lieutenant of Ireland — in which capacity he spent much time in Dublin (and had taken his family with him). Perhaps sensing some feeling of resentment at his father's long absences, the Eighth Duke may have felt that a gesture of some kind was called for.

It should be stressed that local communications were by no means poor. As we have seen, Woodstock was served by two local railheads, and by the 1880s it was possible to reach both Handborough or Woodstock Road by regular omnibus or carrier services. The 1883 *Kelly's Directory*, for example, lists eight local carriers offering services to Oxford, Witney and other destinations; many of these services ran past local stations and it would have been a comparatively easy matter to find cheap (though not quick) transport to a nearby railhead — the gentry would, of course, have used their private gigs or carriages. (As a footnote it is perhaps worth mentioning that in 1881 local road transport had been severely disrupted by heavy snow falls, and towns without rail links had suffered more than places with stations of their own.)

Formation of the Woodstock Railway Company

Whatever his motives the Eighth Duke of Marlborough evidently decided that a rail link between Woodstock and the Oxford & Rugby line was needed, and in 1885 the first plans were tentatively made. It was decided that the new branch line would run eastwards from Woodstock to a junction with the GWR near the village of Shipton-on-Cherwell. The route (which was surveyed by Thomas Berwick) followed Churchill land for most of its 2½ mile length, and it was hoped that the cost of construction would not exceed £10,000 — though in the event this figure was somewhat optimistic.

Plans and sections of the proposed railway were deposited with the Clerk of the Peace at Oxford and with the Borough authorities in Woodstock, while further copies were sent to the relevant authorities in the parishes of Shipton-on-Cherwell, Woodstock and Hensington (though as the Duke was known to be in favour of the new railway it was unlikely that many local people would exercise their right to lodge objections to the proposals!). The projected line ran through agricultural land for much of its length, and only in Woodstock did it interfere with the Duke's tenants; here, the suggested route penetrated a built-up area, and, in an attempt to provide a centrally-sited station, one of the town's medieval 'burgage plots' would be cleared of its existing tenants. The land in question had been sub-divided into various properties and was, in 1885, occupied by the families of William Heynes and Joseph Smith; Joseph Smith would lose his dwelling house, but the unfortunate Heynes family were placed in an even worse position, and would have to give up their dwelling house, garden, orchard and privy.

The Woodstock Railway Bill was presented to Parliament in the early months of 1886, and on 1st February the *Journal of the House of Commons* noted that 'the Chairman of the Select Committee on Standing Orders . . . had conferred with the Chairman of Committees of the House of Lords' for the purpose of determining in which House of Parliament the Bill would be considered, and had decided that it 'should originate in the House of Lords'. This was of course a mere formality, and there was every reason to believe that the Bill would have an easy passage; having been passed by the Upper House it was read for the first time in the House of Commons on 5th April 1886, and then referred to the Examiners of Petitions for Private Bills. The Bill was read for the second time on Wednesday, 16th June 1886, and eight days later the Speaker 'laid upon the table' a report from the Examiners of Petitions for Private Bills stating that the Woodstock Railway Bill and other Bills originating in the House of Lords had complied with Standing Orders.

It seemed that the Bill was soon to receive the Royal Assent, but unfortunately more important events intervened before the Parliamentary process could be brought to fruition. The Liberal government, led by Mr Gladstone, was determined to pass a controversial Home Rule Bill giving partial autonomy to Ireland, but the concept of 'Home Rule' was deeply offensive to many patriotic Englishmen, and in June 1886 Gladstone was defeated by a mass defection of his own supporters. The result of this sensational split in Liberal Party ranks was Gladstone's resignation, and in his place the Queen called upon Lord Salisbury and the Tories to form the next government.

The new 'Caretaker Government' was expected to last only until a General Election (to be held under the extended franchise introduced in 1884) had taken place, but in the meantime Lord Salisbury's administration was faced with a backlog of legislation from the previous session. This was not in the event a major problem and unimportant matters such as the Woodstock Railway Bill were hurried through; on 7th September the House of Commons proceeded to 'take into consideration the Woodstock Bill' and ordered that it should be read for the third time. This was done just three days later, and the Bill was returned to the Upper House 'without amendment'. The complex Parliamentary process was concluded on Saturday, 25th September, when the following message was delivered to the House of Commons by Sir James Drummond, Gentleman Usher of the Black Rod:

> 'Mr Speaker,
> The Lords, authorised by virtue of her Majesty's Commissions for declaring her Royal Assent to several Acts agreed upon by both Houses, and for prolonging the present Parliament, desire the immediate attendance of this Honourable House in the House of Peers, to hear the Commissions read.'

The Speaker, together with those MPs still sitting in the House, then went up to the House of Lords to hear the Royal Assent given to some sixty Acts, of which the Woodstock Railway Act was number thirty-five.

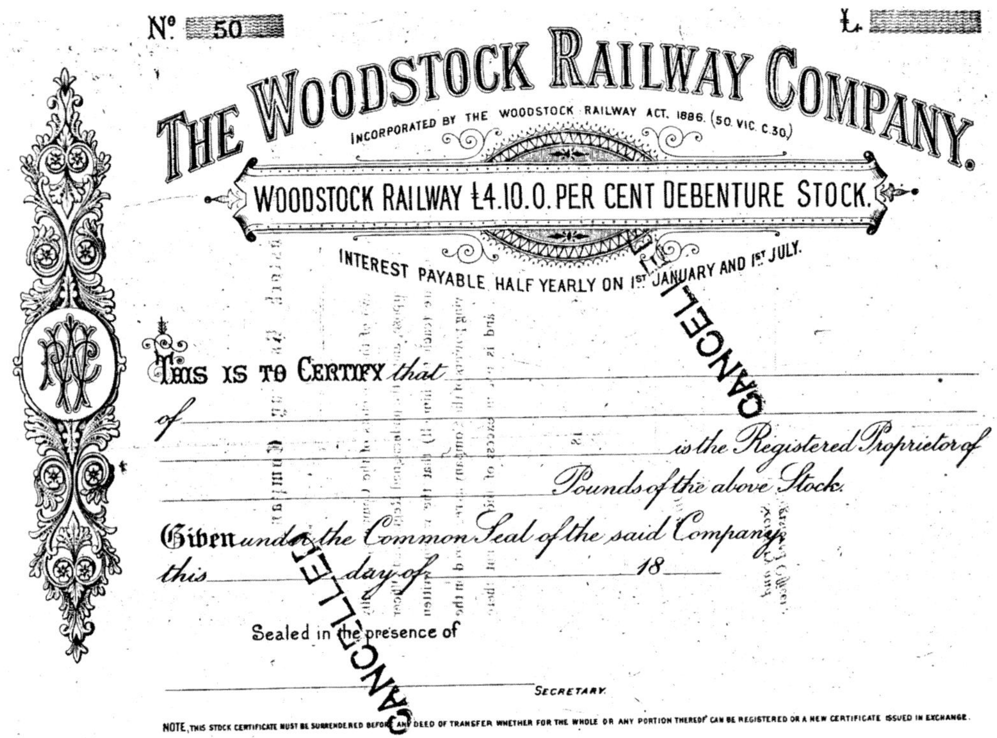

No 50 £

THE WOODSTOCK RAILWAY COMPANY.

INCORPORATED BY THE WOODSTOCK RAILWAY ACT, 1886. (50 VIC. C.30.)

WOODSTOCK RAILWAY £4.10.0. PER CENT DEBENTURE STOCK.

INTEREST PAYABLE HALF YEARLY ON 1ST JANUARY AND 1ST JULY.

CANCELLED

This is to Certify that

of

is the Registered Proprietor of

Pounds of the above Stock.

Given under the Common Seal of the said Company

this day of 18

Sealed in the presence of

CANCELLED

SECRETARY.

NOTE, THIS STOCK CERTIFICATE MUST BE SURRENDERED BEFORE ANY DEED OF TRANSFER WHETHER FOR THE WHOLE OR ANY PORTION THEREOF CAN BE REGISTERED OR A NEW CERTIFICATE ISSUED IN EXCHANGE.

A sample Woodstock Railway share certificate; in fact, the Woodstock Company did not have large numbers of shareholders, and most of its capital was concentrated in the hands of Lucas & Aird or their nominees.

Details of the Act

The newly-passed Act (50 Vic. cap 30) empowered the company to construct a railway 'two miles four furlongs and seven chains in length commencing in the Parish of Shipton-on-Cherwell by a junction with the Great Western Railway . . . one hundred and forty five yards or thereabouts measured in a southerly direction along the said railway from the mile post denoting seventy and a quarter miles from London'. From Shipton the authorised route ascended towards Woodstock, crossing first the Oxford Canal and then the Oxford to Banbury road before terminating 'in the parish of Hensington on or near the eastern edge of the road leading from Woodstock to Oxford in . . . premises forming part of the Blenheim estates in the occupation of the representatives of the late William Heynes, Joseph Smith and George Warmington'. The Woodstock Railway's capital would be £30,000 in three thousand £10 shares, and, if necessary, the company was authorised to borrow up to £10,000. A time limit of three years was set for completion of the works, and there would initially be five directors, all of whom would hold not less than thirty shares. 'The Most Noble George Charles Duke of Marlborough, Sir Francis Bolton and Henry Pratt' were mentioned by name as potential Board members, and these three persons would nominate two further directors or as many others as were deemed necessary.

The Act also went into great detail with respect to the various categories of traffic that might be carried on the Woodstock Railway, and the charges which would be made for each item; 'dung compost and all sorts of manure lime and limestone', for example, would be charged at the rate of one penny per ton per mile, but 'if conveyed in carriages belonging to the company' an additional three farthings would be charged. Similarly, 'all ironstone, iron ore, coal, coke, cinders, bricks, sand, fireclay, slag, dressed stone, salt, tiles, slates, culm and charcoal' would be charged at a rate of one penny farthing per ton per mile, but if conveyed in the company's own vehicles an additional sum not exceeding 2d would be charged.

As far as passengers were concerned, it was stated that the maximum rate of charge to be made by the company 'including the tolls for the use of the railway and of carriages and locomotive power' would be no more than 3d first class, 2d second class and 1d third class. Each traveller would be allowed to take with him 'ordinary luggage not exceeding one hundred and twenty pounds in weight for first class passengers, one hundred pounds in weight for second class passengers and sixty pounds in weight for third class passengers'. These provisions were really legal formalities — which would not in any case concern the Woodstock Railway Company because all train services would be provided by the GWR. It should perhaps be pointed out that identical or near-identical provisions were inserted into many other branch line Acts passed in the latter part of the 19th century.

An Agreement with the GWR

The promoters had not been idle while their Bill was before Parliament, and in March 1886 a draft working agreement was tentatively submitted to the GWR Board. It was suggested that the Great Western might work the Woodstock branch in return for an annual payment of £1,090, leaving the local company with responsibility for staffing the line and maintaining its permanent way; the Woodstock promoters would agree to a defined amount of rolling stock, and there would be 'not more than five trains a day . . . for the conveyance of . . . local and through traffic'. The working agreement was approved by the Great Western directors on 31st March, and authority was given for the common seal of the GW company to be affixed when the full arrangements were completed.

An important meeting of the Woodstock Railway Company was held at 37 Great George Street, Westminster on Friday, 24th February 1888. This apparently innocuous London address was, in reality, highly significant, for 37 Great George Street was the London headquarters of Messrs Lucas & Aird, the well-known contractors. Formed in 1860, Lucas & Aird was a partnership between Charles Lucas and John Aird — a Scottish crofter who had set up a building business in London. It is likely that Lucas & Aird had been involved with the Woodstock Railway from its very inception, and these successful and long-established contractors would no doubt have advised the Churchills on all matters relating to the proposed railway. Indeed, the younger John Aird must have been well-known to Lord Randolph Churchill, for in 1886 Lord Randolph had become MP for South Paddington, and a few months later Aird was elected as Tory MP for neighbouring North Paddington. There was nothing unduly sinister or underhand in any of this; the Churchills were amateurs where railways were concerned and must have welcomed help and advice from John Aird — if John Aird shared some of their political aims and aspirations then so much the better! In the days when momentous national decisions were taken behind the closed doors of a few great houses it was only to be expected that minor decisions affecting a local railway would be made in the same way.

The first meeting was chaired, appropriately enough, by the Duke of Marlborough, and others present included John Alexander Mainly Cope, James Murray, Company Secretary W.F. Woods, Engineer Alfred Priestley, and various representatives from the company's solicitors and bankers. Having obtained their Act, the promoters were able to organise themselves as a properly-constituted company, with the Duke as Chairman and Mr Cope and Mr Murray as directors. Although John Aird and Charles Lucas were not present at this first meeting, many of those taking part were their friends or business associates. Alfred Priestley, for example, was paid not by the Woodstock Railway Company but by Lucas & Aird, while William Fountain Woods was also closely involved with the contractors (his address was given as 37 Great George Street suggesting that he was an employee of John Aird or his partner). Few of those attending this first meeting of the Woodstock Railway Company were Woodstock people, and indeed, it would be true to say that the company lacked any broadly-based, local support.

Sir Francis John Bolton, one of the three directors nominated in the Act, had unfortunately died before taking his place on the Board, and George Lindsay Watson of Blenheim was elected in his place. Watson, an 'estate agent', did at least have some local associations, but his fellow directors were nominees of the contractors and both were London residents, J. Mainly Cope (a solicitor) being based at 14 Pembridge Square, while Mr Murray's address was given as 25 Portman Street.

The newly-constituted Board of Directors concluded their first meeting with a suspiciously brief consideration of a proposed construction contract that had, that very day, been drawn up by Lucas & Aird. The Woodstock Railway minute book makes no mention of any discussion or argument on this important subject, and it seems that the directors affixed their seal to the contract without even reading it — the whole operation had clearly been pre-arranged by Messrs Lucas & Aird and the Duke.

The contract itself was a straightforward document which, from the contractors' point of view, presented few problems. It was conveniently vague *vis-à-vis* materials to be used and the contractors would — through their employee Alfred Priestley — be ultimately responsible for their own quality control. The line would be completed 'in a condition suitable for the conveyance of passenger and goods traffic . . . within the period of six calendar months' and after its inspection by the Board of Trade the contractors agreed to 'deliver up' the railway to the company. There were ample provisions designed to protect Lucas & Aird in the event of 'strikes of workmen or other causes beyond their control' and as usual (in those days) the contractors would be under an obligation to provide:

> '. . . at their own expense all labour, services . . . tools, scaffolding, staging, centreing implements, utensils, machinery, plant and power of every kind and description necessary for the full, safe, expeditious and proper carrying on and completion of the Railway and Works, and also all materials and things of whatever kind . . . required for the due and proper construction and completion of the Railway and Works.'

Another clause dealt with maintenance of the branch in the months following completion, and it was agreed that Lucas & Aird would:

> '. . . at their own expense throughout the progress of the railway and works and until twelve calendar months after the same have been completed and delivered up to the Company . . . maintain the Railway and Works and every part thereof in good and proper order, repair and condition and to the satisfaction in all aspects of the Company's Engineer.'

The contract was, in most respects, similar to many other late Victorian railway construction agreements, but there was a clause relating to financial arrangements which may be worth quoting in full. It provided that Lucas & Aird would:

> '. . . forthwith subscribe for the thirty thousand pounds authorised share capital of the Company and . . . from time to time pay up the sums payable thereon which shall be arranged to be payable at such times and in such amounts as shall correspond with the payments to be made to the contractors . . . but . . . when one half thereof have been paid up the next payment to the contractors shall be made out of the proceeds of the ten thousand pounds Debenture Capital of the Company, and as long as such proceeds shall suffice for such payments no further payments by the contractor on account of the shares shall be required . . . the sum of five thousand pounds shall be paid to them immediately on their commencing the Works as an advance in respect of the plant to be supplied by them for the purposes of the contract and the residue of the said contract price shall be paid in six monthly instalments.'

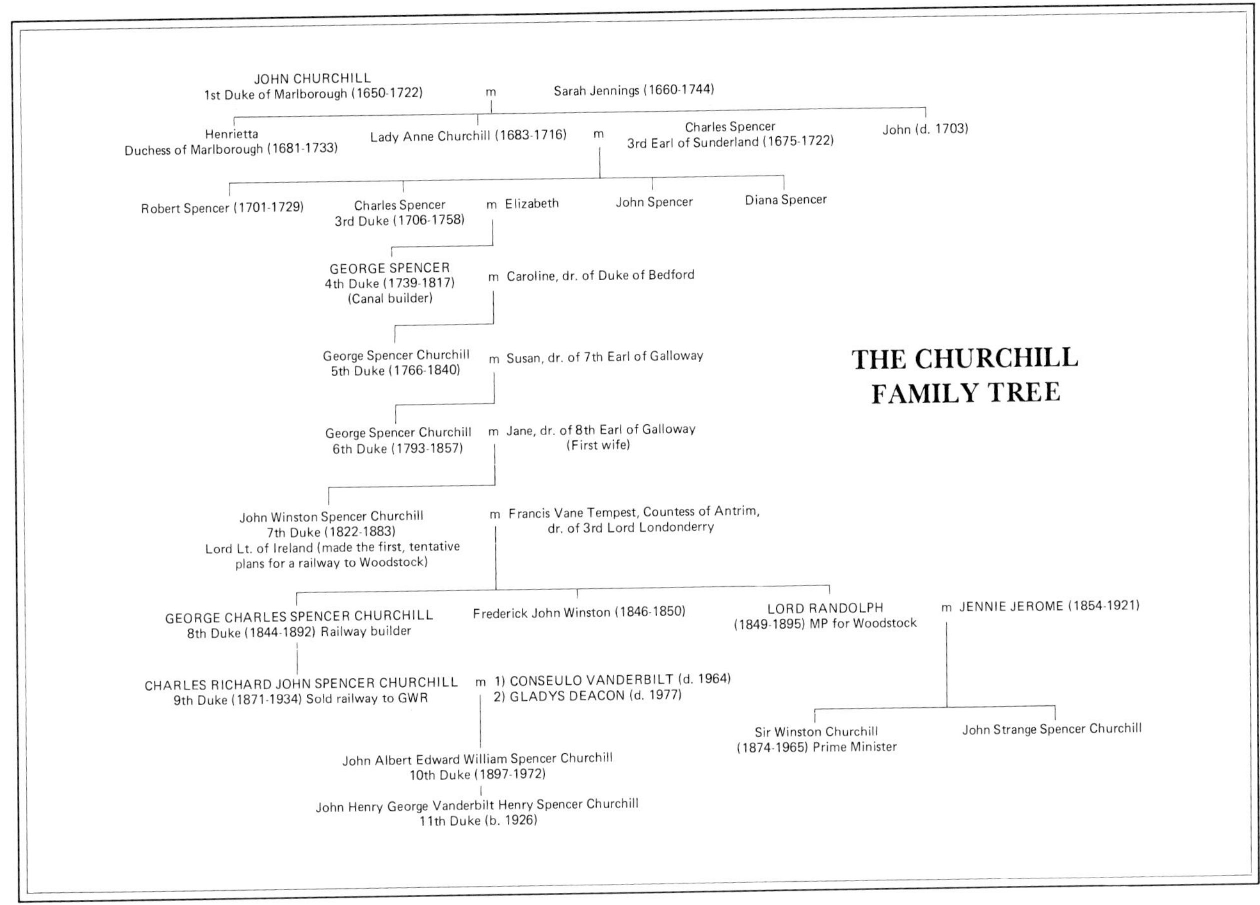

In simple terms, the contract stated that Lucas & Aird would be paid not in cash but in shares — the idea being that only a portion of the authorised £30,000 worth of shares and £10,000 in loans would actually change hands in the form of hard cash.

However, it seems that the full details of this complex financial arrangement were not included in the contract itself and significantly a *further* document (bearing the same date as the main contract) reveals that the Trustees of the Blenheim Estates had agreed to pay to the contractor two-thirds of the sum which the contractor was required to pay 'until the sum of £10,000' had been paid. Moreover, it was also agreed that 'if and when' it was practicable, the parties involved would obtain a further Act in order to create two sets of Woodstock Railway shares; these would be designated 'Series A' and 'Series B', and divided between Lucas & Aird and the Trustees respectively. It was further proposed that Series A shares would eventually yield a preferential dividend of 5%, whereas the holders of Series B shares would not be entitled to a dividend in any one year 'until the full 5% dividend for such year had been paid on Series A'.

The directors held a further meeting at 37 Great George Street on 26th March 1889, with J. Mainly Cope in the chair, and James Murray, Charles Lucas, John Aird, W.F. Woods and others in attendance. There had, in the meantime, been several boardroom changes and Henry Pratt, who had also been listed in the Act, was now a director of the Woodstock Railway. Another newcomer, Mr Robert Swanson Robb, was elected to the board during the meeting, but the main item on the agenda was the creation of £10,000 worth of 4½% debenture shares. This important item of business was discussed at an 'Extraordinary Meeting' which followed the ordinary meeting, and, having agreed to issue these new shares, the directors held a further board meeting at which any remaining matters were discussed.

There can be little doubt that Lucas & Aird were by this time exercising considerable influence over the Duke of Marlborough, the Woodstock Railway, and its Board of Directors. Unfortunately, George, the Eighth Duke was, by temperament, unfit to run a railway company or indeed any other business. Improvident — perhaps slightly eccentric — he had commenced selling heirlooms in an attempt to pay off his many debts. This had in turn prompted a quarrel with Lord Randolph (who felt that the inheritance was being squandered) and by 1889 the two brothers were not on speaking terms. In any case, when the family borough became disfranchised, Randolph had less reason to spend lengthy periods at Blenheim, and under these circumstances George had nobody to turn to for advice on financial and other matters relating to the new railway — apart, that is, from John Aird. Arguably, the contractor may not always have given his aristocratic patron the right kind of advice, and there would be considerable trouble in the coming months. This, however, was in the future, and what mattered in 1889 was that Woodstock would at long last get its railway.

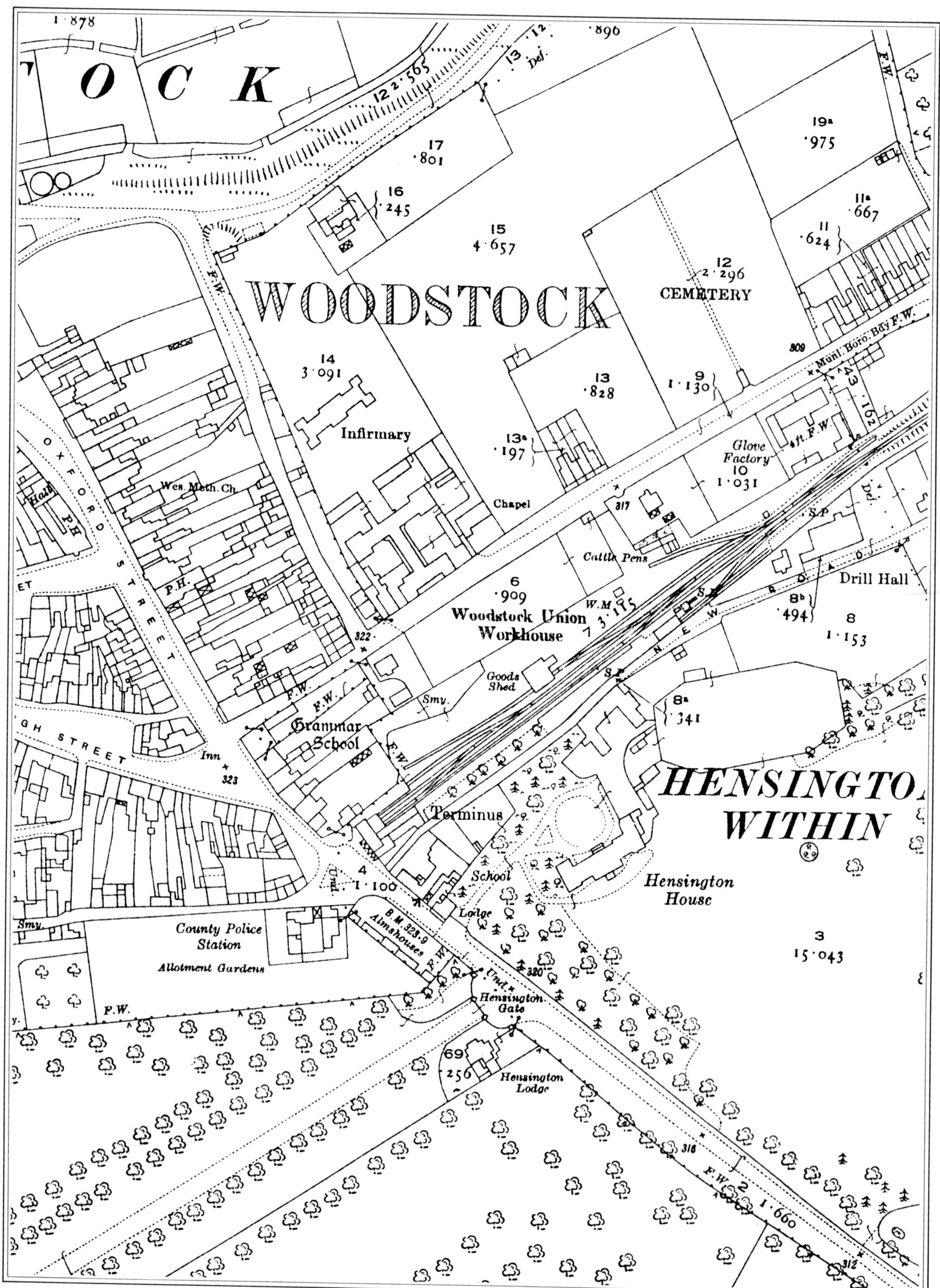

Taken from 25 inch Ordnance Survey c.1898. Crown copyright reserved.

CHAPTER TWO

CONSTRUCTION OF THE WOODSTOCK RAILWAY (1888–1890)

CONSTRUCTION of the 2½ mile single track branch commenced in March 1888, and, in view of the relatively easy nature of their task, experienced contractors such as Messrs Lucas & Aird should have made rapid progress. Leaving its junction with the Oxford & Rugby line at Shipton-on-Cherwell, the authorised route ran through gently rolling countryside with an average elevation of about 250 ft. A substantial embankment would be necessary on either side of the Oxford Canal in order to provide sufficient headroom for narrow boats passing beneath the canal bridge, and three further underbridges were required to carry the branch over one main and two minor roads. Other engineering features included three road overbridges and some relatively deep cuttings on the approaches to Woodstock.

Construction Begins

With preliminary work under way, Lucas & Aird moved a large number of men onto the site, and on 31st March 1888 the *Oxford Chronicle* commented on an unusual air of activity in and around Woodstock as the navvies settled in to their temporary lodgings:–

> 'There are many things which indicate that this undertaking will soon be in progress, and things are looking up in the town in consequence. Void houses are being rapidly occupied, and lodging-house keepers are rapidly filling up their vacant beds and apartments. It will give an impetus to the trade here in most respects, and will therefore be gratefully appreciated. It is not probable that the work will commence to any great extent till after the Easter holidays, but as soon as these are over the undertaking will be pushed forward with all possible despatch.'

The heavy works were started in April, and, in an atmosphere of growing optimism, it was announced that the line would be 'complete in six weeks'.

The chosen route entailed considerable engineering work, but there was a good 'mix' of cuttings and embankments and this should have ensured an economic and speedy completion of the work; in theory, spoil from the cuttings would be taken by temporary contractor's railway and then tipped to form the embankments. By 1888, steam navvies and other mechanised equipment had largely superseded the manual work of earlier years, and by analogy with other contracts Lucas & Aird would have made full use of this new equipment on the Woodstock line. Photographs show that at least one Manning Wardle 0–6–0 saddle tank was employed on the contract, and this characteristic contractor's locomotive would have been used to haul tip wagons up and down a 'temporary way' established during the initial phase of construction.

A Poor Track Record

Before starting work on the Woodstock branch Messrs Lucas & Aird had been involved with a much larger railway contract — the Hull & Barnsley line. Opened on 27th July 1885, this Yorkshire line had cost more than its Parliamentary estimate, and, when finally completed (in an atmosphere of acrimony and recrimination), it was one of the most expensive railways ever built in terms of cost per mile. Suspicious minds wondered if Lucas & Aird had deliberately charged more than a fair price, and there had, moreover, been much speculation concerning an 'understanding' between Charles Lucas and the H & B Chairman. It was hinted that Lucas & Aird had obtained the H & B contract by unfair means and, having been given what amounted to a 'blank cheque', had proceeded to bankrupt the company by their exorbitant demands for cash. Although this may have been an over-simplification, the fact remains that Lucas & Aird had charged prices up to 33% higher than anticipated, and under these circumstances their dominant position on the Woodstock Railway Board must, at first glance, be considered with a degree of suspicion. This suspicion increases when one considers that in 1889 these same contractors secured a 'fixed' contract to build the West Highland Railway and then attempted to get more money by claiming that soil excavated by them was more 'rock' than earth (the same claim had been made during construction of the Hull & Barnsley Railway).

In truth, Messrs Lucas & Aird had an appalling track record in terms of poor cost control, and one feels that if the Churchills had been fully aware of what had happened on the Hull & Barnsley line they would never have let these same contractors start work on the Woodstock branch. On the other hand, John Aird and Charles Lucas were both personally involved with the Woodstock project (being investors as opposed to mere contractors) and this should in theory have ensured a rapid and speedy completion of the contract. Furthermore, John Aird would not wish to do anything which might jeopardise his own advancement up the social ladder — and there can be no doubt that being a friend and business confidant of the Churchills conferred many advantages on this crofter's son. John Aird and his partner therefore took an unusually active part in the affairs of the Woodstock Railway Company, and whatever may or may not have happened on the Hull & Barnsley contract, it seems that the contractors tried as hard as they could to fulfil their obligations to the Duke of Marlborough.

The works proceeded without incident throughout the early months of 1888, and local newspaper reporters commented favourably on Messrs Lucas & Aird's organisational abilities and their enlightened attitude towards those employed on the line. The *Oxfordshire Weekly News* was certainly impressed, and on 10th May 1888 it printed the following report:–

> 'Lucas & Aird are making rapid progress with this line of railway. Temporary metals for the conveyance of materials, etc. have been laid the whole distance, and the greater portion of the fencing is erected, and we understand that the building of the station will be commenced in about two months time. Owing to the large number of navvies engaged at the work it is proposed to employ a scripture reader from the 'Navvies Mission Society', to work amongst the men, visit them on the works, and hold classes, night

schools, etc. The stipend of the scripture reader for the half year will be £26, and other expenses, towards which the contractors . . . will contribute £10.'

It is likely that the railway was substantially complete by 1889, but, sadly, various unspecified problems prevented an early opening of the branch. Company minutes provide no real insight into the nature of these difficulties, but it is possible that a period of heavy rain in the spring of 1889 had caused problems with the newly-formed earthworks. To be fair to Lucas & Aird, it was exceedingly difficult to build embankments during persistent rain, and few contractors could have accomplished their task on time under such trying conditions. However, in the case of the Woodstock branch there were rumours of deeper problems, and many local people began to feel that the project would not be brought to fruition. It seemed that the company was becoming a laughing stock, and press reports became openly sarcastic. On 4th May 1889, for example, the following note appeared in the *Oxford Chronicle* under the heading 'Woodstock Railway':–

'One or two conflicting rumours are afloat as to when and how this undertaking will be completed, but in the absence of any direct corroberation it would be premature to say further. One thing is certain, that very nearly all the hands have been discharged and little progress is being made, and whether or not there will be railway communication opened from the town to Oxford this year is an open question.'

The press and public simply could not understand why the railway remained unfinished, and, for reasons best known to themselves, the Woodstock Railway directors made very little attempt to explain their motives for abandoning the partially-finished line. In fact, the impediment was caused not by engineering problems or financial difficulties but by a fundamental difference of opinion between the Woodstock Railway and the GWR, and at the root of this whole dispute was the junction at Woodstock Road. Indeed, this relatively simple matter almost wrecked the entire scheme — but, before examining the problem in detail, it is necessary to outline some further boardroom changes that took place between March 1889 and March 1890.

The Woodstock Railway's directors, in March 1889, included John Alexander Mainly Cope, James Murray, the Duke of Marlborough, John Aird, Henry Pratt, George Lindsay Watson, and Robert Swanson Robb. Apart from John Aird and the Duke, these gentlemen took little interest in the railway, and most of them were merely nominal directors whose names were used to add weight to the company. Henry Pratt resigned by March 1890, and George Lindsay Watson had died, but John William Palmer was elected in place of Mr Watson, and Charles Lucas was subsequently brought in as a replacement for Mr Pratt.

In practice, Lucas had, with his partner, been a dominant figure in the company since its inception, and the two contractors were intimately involved in all aspects of company policy. They had, for instance, approved the working agreement under which the GWR would operate the branch in return for a share of the profits. This agreement was formally submitted to the Woodstock Railway Board on 6th May 1889 but unfortunately, the agreement could not be put into effect until the railway was open to traffic — and that in turn was subject to a satisfactory outcome of the Woodstock Road dispute.

The Problems at Woodstock Road

There was, at the outset, no problem at all, and the terms of the Woodstock Railway Bill seemed to indicate that Woodstock Railway trains would have a clear right of access over the GWR to Woodstock Road station. The appropriate part of the Bill may be worth quoting. It provided that:–

'The Company and all Companies and persons lawfully working or using the railway of the Company or any part thereof may run over and use with their engines and carriages of every description and with their officers and servants and for the purposes of traffic of every description the portion of Railway following (that is to say):– So much of the Great Western Railway as is situate and lies between the junction therewith of the railway and the Woodstock Road Station of the Great Western Railway. Together with that and all platforms, sidings, roads, watering places, water supply, booking and other offices, waterhouses, landing places, signals, points, buildings, machinery, works and conveniences on or connected therewith respectively, and the Companies owning or working the said portion of Railway and stations shall afford all requisite facilities for the purpose.'

The precise wording of this provision suggests that Woodstock branch trains would run over the Great Western main line in order to reach Woodstock Road station, and there is no reason to suppose that the Duke of Marlborough, or his adviser John Aird, ever considered building a separate junction station at Shipton-on-Cherwell; the Woodstock Railway's authorised capital would not, in any case, have allowed such a facility. However, the GWR was unwilling to let branch trains run over the main line, and when the Woodstock Bill was passed *the vital clause relating to running powers was omitted*. The full implications of this omission only became clear when the Great Western unexpectedly insisted that a junction station was needed at Shipton-on-Cherwell.

The matter was raised at a GWR Board meeting on 25th November 1888, when the Great Western General Manager mentioned 'a difficulty' which had arisen in connection with the Woodstock Railway 'owing to no provision having been made in the capital required for its construction, either for a proper station at the junction or for the work required at Woodstock Road station'. The General Manager's choice of words placed the blame for this problem firmly on the local company, but in fairness to John Aird, there was no obvious reason why Woodstock branch trains should not have run over the short section of line between Woodstock Road station and the junction at Shipton-on-Cherwell. Money for an extra platform for branch trains at Woodstock Road would no doubt have been forthcoming from the Woodstock Railway, but this course of action did not satisfy the Great Western, and there was instead a suggestion that in lieu of the junction proposed at Shipton-on-Cherwell the branch could be carried, for about a mile, along the western side of the GWR main line 'so as to bring trains to and from the Woodstock line directly into the Woodstock Road station'.

The Woodstock directors (who may have envisaged trains running through to Oxford) were unable to pay for such an extension of their authorised line, and asked if the GWR would be prepared to advance sufficient capital — the figure suggested being about £11,000. In return, the local company offered to pay interest upon the amount required at a 'rate of not less than 8% per annum'. After discussion, the Great Western Board seemed amenable to the idea of helping to pay for the proposed extension, and Mr Lambert, the General Manager, was authorised to enter into negotiations with the Woodstock Railway Company.

A meeting was later arranged between Henry Lambert, John Aird and the Duke of Marlborough, and on 21st March 1889 Lambert, reporting back to his Board, stated that the Woodstock Railway directors were prepared to contribute £4,137 towards a total of £9,650 which would be needed to construct a third line into Woodstock Road station and carry out the necessary platform alterations there. The Great Western would have to find the balance of £5,513, but the Woodstock Company had agreed to pay the sum of £150 a year towards the cost of maintaining the third line between Shipton-on-Cherwell and Woodstock Road.

Sadly, even this limited payment proved too much for the local company, and on 23rd May the Great Western Board members were told that it was impossible for the Woodstock Railway to make any further advance or give security in respect of the agreed payment of £150 per annum. After a discussion the Great Western directors resolved that £150 could be paid out of traffic receipts once the branch was in operation (this would be in addition to the sum of £1,090 which the Woodstock Railway had agreed to pay in respect of locomotives and rolling stock).

It was decided that Messrs Lucas & Aird would construct the extra works between Shipton-on-Cherwell and Woodstock Road station, with W. Lancaster Owen acting as engineer on behalf of the GWR. The Great Western also agreed to purchase any switches, crossings or other permanent way materials that had already been provided by the Woodstock Railway for use at the now-abandoned junction at Shipton. The schedule for these additional works was as follows:–

> 'Construction of line from point of junction with the Woodstock line to the Woodstock Road Station and laying of permanent way, but exclusive of materials.
>
> Extension of 300 feet of Down platform in the Woodstock Road Station.'

Lucas & Aird's payment would be £5,497, subject to land being acquired on satisfactory terms (and also to the completion of an agreement with the Woodstock Railway Company). Other expenditure incurred by the GWR would be an estimated £2,577 for permanent way materials, £202 for alterations in the siding arrangements at Woodstock Road, and £1,285 for locking and signalling. Some extra portions of land would be required, and on 10th July 1889 it was reported that negotiations were in progress with the Oxford Canal Company, with Wadham College and with Exeter College; there were minor problems with the latter, but the matter was finally sorted out when the college authorities suggested that they could give up a part of a disputed piece of land if the GWR would surrender its interest in some property that was not required for the extra line.

In contrast to the earlier delays, Lucas & Aird made good progress on the 'third line' section between Woodstock Road and Shipton-on-Cherwell, and the work of 'widening' was accomplished between November 1889 and March or April 1890. It is true that the former Oxford & Rugby line (being a former double track broad gauge route) provided ample room for a third line of rails beside the main up and down line, but, on the other hand, the contractors had to contend with two river crossings in less than half a mile. Nevertheless, the massive bridge girders were in place by the early months of 1890, and the Woodstock branch was finally completed in the following spring.

A Further Act of Parliament

The third line between Shipton and Woodstock Road was built on Great Western land, and it was unnecessary to obtain specific Parliamentary consent; the Great Western nevertheless inserted some Woodstock provisions into a comprehensive General Powers Bill which was submitted to Parliament in the early months of 1890. This new Bill sought to confer further powers upon the GWR for the vesting in Great Western ownership of the Whitland & Cardigan Railway and other companies, while at the same time seeking consent for an extension of time for the Woodstock Railway to complete its works.

The most important part of the Bill, as far as the Woodstock Railway was concerned, was the section asking permission to alter the junction arrangements at Shipton-on-Cherwell. When passed, the General Powers Act enabled the Great Western to build an independent line of rails '1 mile 6 chains 23 links' in length and 'commencing in the Parish of Shipton-on-Cherwell in the County of Oxford, about 4 chains southwards from the southern end of the bridge carrying the said railway over the Oxford Canal and terminating in the Parish of Kidlington . . . at the Woodstock Road station'. The junction authorised at Shipton-on-Cherwell would be abandoned, but the Great Western agreed to construct the new line in its place and also 'carry out and complete such alterations in the Woodstock Road station as may be necessary to accommodate the traffic of the Woodstock Company'. These belated changes of plan increased the length of the branch by just over a mile, the distance between Woodstock Road station and the buffers at Woodstock being 3 miles 57 chains.

The 1890 General Powers Act contained several other provisions relating to the Woodstock branch, and in addition to dealing with the new junction and granting the Woodstock company an extension of time, the new Act also confirmed the operating agreement between the two companies. Indeed, this earlier agreement was legally clarified by the new Act — which dealt with the relationship between the Woodstock Railway and the GWR in great detail and was clearly designed as a definitive statement of mutual responsibilities. As such, it would be interesting to examine the 1890 Act in greater detail with particular reference to the clauses relating to operation.

Some Details of the 1890 Act

The new branch line was to be completed as a single standard gauge railway, with 'proper and sufficient station fittings, furniture, sheds, cranes, water, signals, electric telegraph, and other works . . . together with an engine shed, a weighbridge, a water tank and a water crane'. When 'passed by the inspecting officer of the Board of Trade as being in all respects fit to be opened and used for public traffic' the Great Western would have 'full right and power at all times . . . to pass over and use the railway and all sidings, stations, appurtenances works and conveniences . . . with engines and carriages of every description'.

Unusually, the Act specified the type and quantity of rolling stock to be used on the branch, and the GW was to provide 'one engine, one van, one long composite carriage consisting of 1st 2nd and 3rd class compartments, and one third class carriage, and all necessary fuel and water, and the requisite staff of engine drivers and stokers for the due and proper carrying of traffic of all kinds over the railway, and when and as required for the purposes of any such traffic will also provide one extra composite carriage, one horse box, one carriage truck and twelve goods trucks' (!).

Other provisions in this clearly defined working agreement dealt with ownership of the 'third line' between Shipton-on-Cherwell and Woodstock Road, payments to be made by the Woodstock company to the GWR, and distribution of profits:–

(2) The Woodstock Company shall for the purposes of the said third line of rails vest or cause to be vested in the Great Western Company in fee simple and without compensation the strip of land delineated and coloured red on the . . . plan hereto annexed containing 1 rood and 28 perches or thereabouts, and shall contribute and pay to the Great Western Railway Company upon the execution of these presents and before the works to be constructed by them under this agreement are commenced the sum of £4,130 towards the expense to be incurred by the Great Western Company in the construction of such works, and upon such payment the Great Western Company shall construct and complete the said works with all reasonable despatch.

(4) In consideration of, and as one of the conditions of such privilege, the Great Western will in the exercise of such running powers carry over the railway for the Woodstock Company not only such traffic (goods as well as passengers) from or to any station on the railway, but also the traffic arising and terminating on the railway at Woodstock, and will carry all such traffic with regularity and expedition, and in all respects as if such traffic were their own proper traffic upon one of their own branch lines, and from the date of this agreement the Woodstock Company shall not themselves exercise or grant to any Company or person any right or privilege over or upon the railway inconsistent with, or which may directly or indirectly impede or interfere with the use and enjoyment by the Great Western Company of any of the rights, powers, and privileges intended to be secured to them by this agreement.

(6) The Great Western Company will, until it shall be otherwise agreed or determined by arbitration, run over the railway five trains each way daily (Sundays, Christmas Day and Good Friday excepted) at such hours as shall be reasonably convenient for the accommodation of the traffic, and in the event of the directors of the Woodstock Company objecting to the times at which such trains may be run or requiring any increased number of trains to be run, the question of the times and of the increased payment to be made to the Great Western Company shall be determined by arbitration in the manner hereinafter provided. Provided always that in any arbitration as to the increased payment to be made to the Great Western Company, that Company shall always be entitled, having regard to the cost incurred by them for the purposes of this agreement, to receive £150 per annum over and above the amount which the arbitrator may award to be paid in respect of the train service, that is to say, the amount which, for the purposes of any such arbitration the arbitor shall be entitled to consider as the cost of the train service under this agreement, shall be the sum of £1,090, but the Great Western Company shall be entitled to receive £150 over and above the increased amount which the arbitrator may award in the same manner as they receive £1,240 under this agreement.

(7) The directors of the Woodstock Company shall fix the rates and fares for the local traffic on the railway, and the directors of the Great Western Company shall fix rates and fares for the through traffic.

(8) The Woodstock Company shall, at their own expense, keep and maintain the railway in an efficient state of repair for the exercise by the Great Western Company of the running powers hereby granted to that Company, and they shall also provide at their own expense the necessary station master, clerks, porters, signalmen and other staff required for the conduct of the traffic on the railway, and all stores stationery, tickets, materials and appliances necessary for the efficient maintenance and working of the railway.

(9) When, and as soon as, the net divisible profits of the Woodstock Company amount to such a sum as would be sufficient to pay a dividend at the rate of £3 per cent per annum upon the whole of the then share capital of the Woodstock Company, the Woodstock Company shall further pay the Great Western Company for the use of their station at Woodstock Road and for any services performed by the Great Western Company in respect of the traffic of the Woodstock Company there the fixed sum of £100 per annum, the Woodstock Road Station being considered . . . for the purposes of traffic . . . passing only over the Woodstock Railway, a station upon that railway.

(10) In the event of the Woodstock Company failing to perform the obligations undertaken by them under this agreement, it shall be in the option of the Great Western Company . . . to . . . do and perform any matter in which the Woodstock Company may make default with liberty, if the Great Western Company so think fit, to deduct any expense so incurred from any moneys coming to the Woodstock Company under this agreement.

(11) In the event of this agreement being determined under the provisions in the last article contained, the Woodstock Company shall be entitled to run over and use the parallel line of the Great Western Company to be constructed under the provisions of this agreement, and the Woodstock Road Station of the Great Western Company on payment of such rent, or failing agreement settled by arbitration.

(12) The gross receipts in respect of the railway from tolls, rates and charges in respect of traffic of all kinds . . . shall . . . be apportioned as follows viz.:–

The Great Western Company shall be entitled to receive out of the gross receipts the sum of £1,240 in each year for conveying in their carriages and wagons over the railway the traffic of the Woodstock Cmpany and the residue or balance shall be retained by the Woodstock Company or be paid over to them by the Great Western Company as the case may be.'

Curiously, the 1890 General Powers Act did not receive the Royal Assent until August 1890 — by which time the Woodstock branch had already been opened to traffic! This was not, however, a major problem; the working agreement, for example, had been signed in the previous November and its inclusion in the Act was merely a formality. Similarly, the powers relating to junction arrangements were formalities rather than legal necessities, while the extension of time (which was not required) was a sensible precautionary measure which would clearly have been useful in the event of legal or other problems.

Meanwhile, with the railway at last completed throughout from Woodstock to the bay platform at Woodstock Road, the

Lucas & Aird's 0–6–0 Manning Wardle locomotive No. 132 stands in the newly completed terminus with what is thought to be Colonel Rich's inspection train. Formed of conventional chaired rail, the track on the Woodstock branch differed from certain of its contemporaries (such as the Staines and Tetbury branches) which were laid with flat-bottomed rail. *Collection P. J. T. Reed*

GWR was able to prepare for opening. On 9th May 1890 the company informed the Board of Trade that the new connections at Woodstock Road were ready for inspection, and on 12th May the BOT replied, stating that Colonel Rich would inspect the new works. In the same month the Woodstock Railway was sent a list of stores provided by the GWR, including books and stationery to the value of £9 10s 4d.

The third line between Woodstock Road and the Woodstock Railway was inspected by Colonel Rich on 14th May 1890. It is easy to imagine that spring day, when Colonel Rich climbed aboard his two-coach special in the new bay platform at Woodstock Road station and Lucas & Aird's open-cabbed saddle tank No 132 set off slowly along the new railway. Running beside the main line the inspection train paused on each of the new bridges before turning sharply westwards onto the branch proper. Heading westwards along towering new embankments the train soon reached the Banbury Road bridge, then continued slowly through raw, grassless cuttings to Woodstock. Here, a small group of onlookers had gathered — including an intrepid Victorian photographer who recorded the historic scene for posterity! Well pleased with what he had seen, the Colonel reported as follows:–

'Sir,

I have the honour to report, for the information of the Board of Trade, that in compliance with the instructions contained in your minute . . . I have inspected the widening (3rd line of rails) from Woodstock Road station on the GW Railway to the junction with the Woodstock Railway.

The new line is a little more than 1 mile long, the gauge is 4 ft 8½ ins and the permanent way is of the Great Western standard pattern for branch lines, and is in good order. The sharpest curve has a radius of 14 chains and the ruling gradient is 1 in 522. The line is well fenced.

The works consist of two old brick bridges over the line, three new under bridges that have wrought iron girders and platforms which are carried on brick abutments, and two viaducts, each of two spans, that carry the railway over the River Cherwell. The viaducts have wrought iron girders and platforms which are carried on brick abutments and piers. The widest span is 50 ft.

Woodstock Road, which has been altered and enlarged, is the only station, as the north end of this single line joins the Woodstock Railway end on.

The junction cabin at Woodstock Road has 39 working and 12 spare levers, which are interlocked. The new bay platform is at the south side of the main down line platform. The field gates require fencing to lead up to the rails, and subject to this being done, I can recommend the Board of Trade to approve the additions and alterations at Woodstock Road station, and sanction the opening of the new line for passenger traffic, as soon as the companies hand in a satisfactory undertaking for working the single line.

I understand that it is to be worked by train staff, in connection with block working.

Yours etc,

Colonel Rich, RE,

With meticulous accuracy, the Colonel treated the Woodstock Road–Shipton and Shipton–Woodstock sections as two distinct railways, and the Woodstock Railway proper was the subject of a separate report:–

'Sir,

I have the honour to report for the information of the Board of Trade, that in compliance with the instructions contained in your

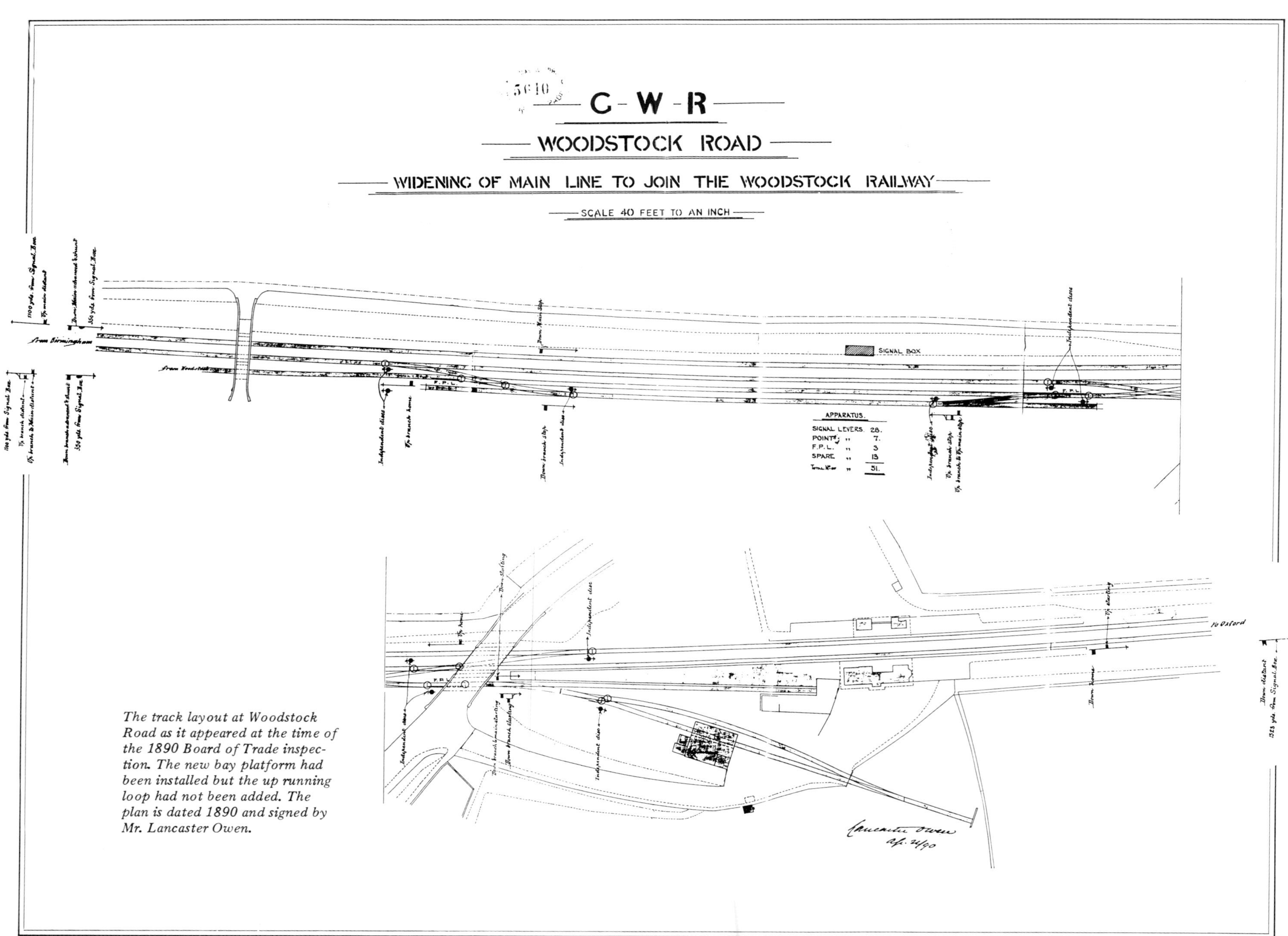

The track layout at Woodstock Road as it appeared at the time of the 1890 Board of Trade inspection. The new bay platform had been installed but the up running loop had not been added. The plan is dated 1890 and signed by Mr. Lancaster Owen.

Another view of the 1890 Board of Trade inspection train. This photograph shows part of the original Woodstock track layout with its single slip (left) and engine shed (left distance). *Collection P. J. T. Reed*

Minute of 23rd ultimo, I have inspected the Woodstock Railway, which commences by a junction end on with the GWR, about a mile north of Woodstock Road Station and extends to the town of Woodstock.

The new railway is a single line on the 4 foot 8½ inch gauge. It is 2 miles 47 chains long. The sharpest curve has a radius of 14 chains and the ruling gradient is 1 in 68.

The permanent way is similar to that adopted for the Great Western Branch Lines and consists of a Bullhead steel rail that weighs 76lbs per yard. It is fished and fixed with outside wooden keys in cast iron chairs that weigh 36 lbs each. The chairs are fixed with two fang bolts to wooden sleepers laid transversely about 2 foot 9 inches apart except those next to the rail joints which are only 2 foot 3 inches apart. The sleepers are 9 feet by 10 inches × 5 inches. The railway is well ballasted with gravel and well fenced with post and rails.

The works consist of two brick, two wooden and one overbridge that has wrought iron girders on brick abutments — four underbridges that have wrought iron girders and platforms that are carried on brick arches.

The only station is Blenheim and Woodstock. The points and signals are worked from a raised cabin at the north end of the yard. No. 1 signal should lock No. 5 points. I enclose undertakings as to the proposed mode of working which is satisfactory, and I can recommend the Board of Trade to sanction the opening of the Woodstock Railway for passenger traffic subject to the above mentioned alteration being made in the locking at Blenheim.

I have etc.
F.H. Rich Col. R.E.'

It is interesting to note that the Colonel's first report contains two apparent errors. The most glaring mistake concerns the position of the new bay platform at Woodstock Road, which was situated not on the south but to the *west* of the main down platform. Of less magnitude is Colonel Rich's description of the 'two old brick bridges'; these were, as far as can be ascertained, built of locally-quarried stone (though they may have incorporated a brick 'core'). Also worthy of further comment is the reference to two viaducts and three under-bridges, which suggests that there were five large bridges on the mile long line. In fact there were just two main bridges, both of which spanned the River Cherwell; the other three bridges carried the railway across farm tracks, all three being little more than cattle creeps with an average span of about 11 ft.

The expensive extension into Woodstock Road station had, needless to say, severely taxed the Woodstock Railway's subscribed capital, but the 4½% debenture stock created in March 1889 had done much to rectify the situation. Even this, however, was insufficient to cover the company's debts and in July 1889 the directors had been obliged to raise a further £8,000. Lucas & Aird had presented engineer's certificates for a total of £20,000 in July 1889 and March 1890, but in practice they had by now accepted debenture stock rather than hard cash, and they were in consequence the largest shareholders in the Woodstock Railway Company.

On Friday 16th May 1890 the GWR presented their formal undertaking as to the mode of working to the Board of Trade, and on Saturday Woodstock residents learned that the railway would be opened to traffic on the following Monday. The third line between Shipton and Woodstock Road would be brought into use concurrently with the branch, and at the same time the latter station would be renamed *Kidlington*. The scene was thus set for a traditional 'Opening Day', which in true Victorian fashion would enable the entire community to celebrate its good fortune in being connected to the outside world after years of stagnation; the age of steam had, after many vicissitudes, at last reached rural Woodstock!

An Edwardian view of Blenheim & Woodstock station, with the Church of England school to the right and horse-drawn delivery vehicles in the foreground; the cart on the left probably belonged to a local carrier (possibly Mary Guy, who, in December 1908, agreed to provide cartage facilities within a mile radius of Woodstock). *Lens of Sutton*

CHAPTER THREE

OPENING AND EARLY YEARS (1890–1897)

HAVING successfully passed its Board of Trade inspection, the Woodstock Railway was ceremonially opened to traffic on Monday, 19th May 1890. Happily, it is possible to reconstruct that momentous occasion with the aid of an eye-witness account which appeared in the *Oxford Times* just six days later.

Opening Day

It seems that the opening came as something of a surprise, and the paper noted somewhat petulantly, that 'contrary to expectation there was no official recognition of the opening on the part of the corporation, although this apparent laxity may have arisen from the fact that until the extreme end of last week, little or nothing had oozed out to lead anyone to suppose that the event would take place'. In spite of this short notice, the local populace had obviously been well-informed, and large numbers of them turned out 'at an early hour to see the first train start from their native town'; they also arrived in large numbers, added the paper, 'to witness the first train arrive at the station'.

The first down working had in fact left Oxford at six o'clock in the morning, with Oxford's station master, Mr R. Davis in charge. Many of those waiting on the platform at Woodstock had already purchased tickets for a ride on the first up service, and these first day travellers included the Mayor of Woodstock — Mr Robert Rowles — and his grandchildren. The first up train left Woodstock 'well filled' with 120 people aboard, and a 'faint cheer' was heard as it steamed out. The next departure carried over 200 travellers, including children, teachers and monitors from the nearby Church of England school who had been given a free ride and a holiday through the 'thoughtful kindness of the Rector, the Reverend A. Majendie and other gentlemen'. This was 'the event of the day' claimed the *Oxford Times* reporter, and 'on the start and on the return the heartiest possible cheers were given by the youngsters in the way that only youngsters can cheer, for the kind friends who had so generously afforded them so great a treat'. Otherwise, continued the paper, 'not a drum was heard, nor a flag seen, either at the station, on the engine, or in the town, and a stranger would never have dreamt that an important event was taking place'.

In all, the railway carried 432 passengers on its first day of operation, including 7 first class, 7 second class and 418 third class travellers. In his conclusion the *Oxford Times* reporter expressed the pious hope that the coming of the railway would 'benefit in a material degree the town and trade of Woodstock'. Finally the reporter offered 'grateful thanks to the Duke of Marlborough' for the efforts he had made to bring 'direct railway communication' to the ancient town of Woodstock.

'A Well-fitted Station'

Opened in the closing years of Victoria's reign, the Woodstock branch was a comparatively modern railway, yet its buildings and other features were of traditional appearance and construction. The terminus in particular exuded a 'period' atmosphere that would have been slightly quaint even in 1890, and in this context it is interesting to compare Woodstock with contemporary Great Western branch termini such as Shipston-on-Stour and Tetbury (both opened in 1889). These two stations were given modest, highly utilitarian pre-fabricated wooden buildings, (indeed the original plans for Woodstock were for a wooden building similar to that erected) but Woodstock, in contrast had an L-shaped,

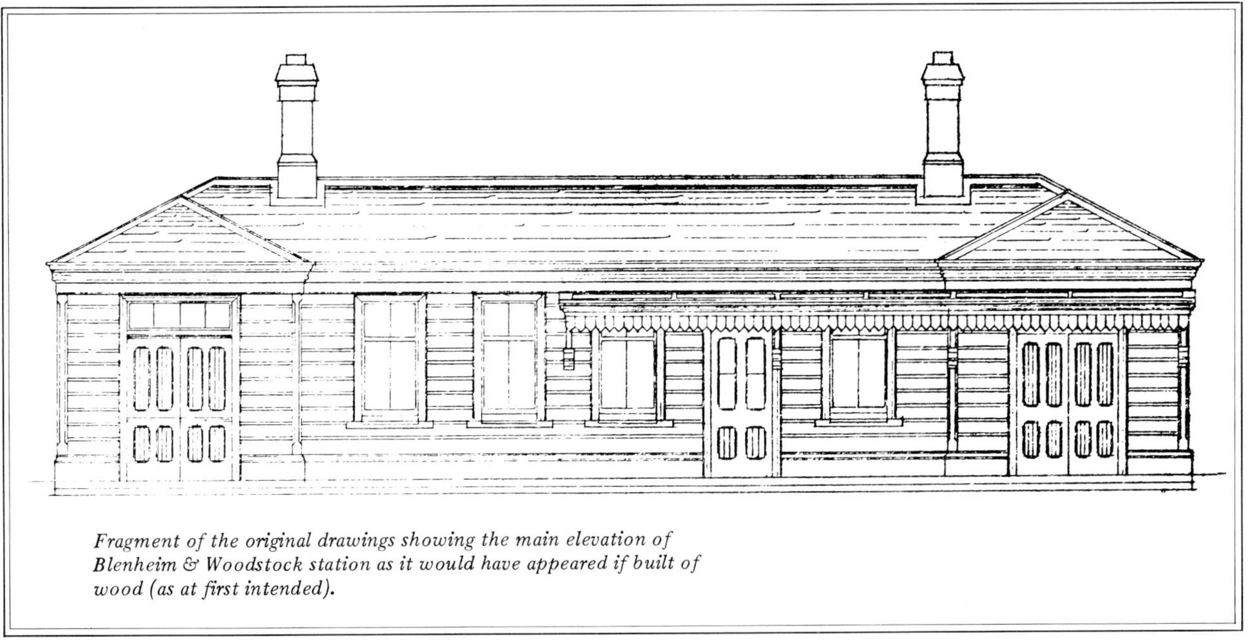

Fragment of the original drawings showing the main elevation of Blenheim & Woodstock station as it would have appeared if built of wood (as at first intended).

hip-roofed terminal building, solidly constructed of local Cotswold stone, and entirely in keeping with its historic surroundings. Although it was clearly a specially designed building, the new station was of recognisably 'Great Western' appearance and might have been categorised as a 'de luxe' version of the company's standard late-Victorian style. A substantially similar L-shaped building had already been provided at Bodmin in 1887, and it is likely that the plans for Woodstock had been traced from the Bodmin drawings. Clearly, no expense had been spared, and the terminus — which was officially called *Blenheim* & Woodstock — was perhaps too grand for the small town that it served. This was certainly the opinion of the *Oxford Times* reporter who called it 'a well-fitted station . . . with all the latest improvements . . . sufficient for a place of much larger size'; no doubt this exceptionally well-built station owed much to the Duke of Marlborough, whose palace was within a stone's throw of the railway.

When first projected, the Woodstock Railway had been designed, not just as a short dead-end branch but as an important excursion destination, capable of handling large numbers of visitors to Blenheim Palace. For this reason the track layout at Woodstock was relatively complex, and consisted basically of three parallel lines, two of which were linked by crossovers to form a run-round loop of approximately 800 feet which could accommodate ten-coach trains with ease. The main goods road passed through a corrugated iron goods shed and finally terminated in a carriage dock, and there was, in addition, a short dead-end siding serving a cattle dock and coal wharves.

The most curious feature of the track layout was a short spur which diverged sharply from the run-round loop and cut across the goods siding before terminating abruptly in a corner of the station yard. It is likely that this spur was installed in connection with horse and carriage traffic; such a feature would have been most useful during the 1890s and early 1900s when the Woodstock branch was used by numerous political or military specials. On the other hand, the spur may have been intended simply as an extra siding for use when the adjacent loading dock was occupied — whatever its original purpose, the spur (and an associated single slip) was an extravagant feature that served no useful purpose and was soon taken out of use.

Other facilities at the new station included a stone-built weigh-house and a corrugated-iron engine shed, together with a small brick-built water tower and an unusually tall wooden signal box. This last-mentioned structure was a hip-roofed box of tower-like dimensions, which nevertheless afforded signalmen an excellent view of the entire terminus (further details of these structures will be found in Chapter Five). Blenheim & Woodstock was fully signalled, with a starter at the end of the platform, an advanced starter at the station throat and a home and distant controlling down traffic; the single line between Woodstock and Kidlington was initially worked by train staff which, as the *Oxford Times* reporter enthusiastically recorded, ensured that no collisions were possible.

In its first months the Blenheim & Woodstock branch was served by five passenger trains each way as specified in the Woodstock Railway's working agreement with the GWR. The June 1890 timetable shows an additional, goods-only working which left Woodstock at 7.30 am (arriving at Kidlington by 7.40 am) but this service was withdrawn in the following July, suggesting that there was insufficient traffic for a separate branch goods service. Goods vehicles were also conveyed by an evening passenger train, which in June 1890 left Woodstock at 8.35 pm. Other services departed from Woodstock at 8.00 am, 11.00 am, 3.00 pm and 6.15 pm, returning from Kidlington at 9.05 am, 12.20 pm, 3.35 pm and 6.35 pm respectively. Local travellers had hoped that all trains would run through to Oxford, but the timetables suggest that most services terminated at Kidlington.

It is surprisingly difficult to identify *which* trains worked through to Oxford during the pre-1900 period, but it seems that, on balance, the first up service from Woodstock may have continued through to Oxford after calling at Kidlington. The June 1890 timetable is vague on this point, but by July 1890 the 8.00 am from Woodstock had become the 8.13 from Kidlington, reaching Oxford by 8.26 am. In the reverse direction the 8.50 am down service definitely continued to Woodstock. By July 1892, the 8.00 pm from Blenheim & Woodstock is clearly shown as a through working, and it is assumed that this train worked back to Woodstock at 8.45 pm. There is however no obvious reason why in 1890 one morning train ran through, whereas by 1892 an *evening* train worked through to Oxford; such an unbalanced distribution of through workings would have been of little use to Woodstock residents, and the most plausible explanation is that for staffing purposes it was necessary for at least one train to reach Oxford. Alternatively, it is possible that locomotives stocked up with a full bunker of coal once a day at Oxford

BLENHEIM AND WOODSTOCK BRANCH.

(WORKED BY TRAIN STAFF.)

Single Line between Blenheim and Woodstock and Kidlington.

Fo m of Staff and Ticket, ROUND; Colour, RED.

DOWN TRAINS—WEEK DAYS.

Distance.	STATIONS.		1 D Goods.	2 A Passenger.	3 A Passenger.	4 A Passenger.	5 A Passenger.	6 A Passenger.
			A.M.	A.M.	P.M.	P.M.	P.M.	P.M.
	Kidlington	dep.	7 30	9 5	12 20	3 35	6 35	8 55
	Blenheim and Woodstock	arr.	7 40	9 15	12 30	3 45	6 45	9 5

UP TRAINS—WEEK DAYS.

Distance.	STATIONS.		1 D Goods.	2 A Passenger.	3 A Passenger.	4 A Passenger.	5 A Passenger.	6 A Mixed.
			A.M.	A.M.	A.M.	P.M.	P.M.	P.M.
	Blenheim and Woodstock	dep.	7 0	8 0	11 0	3 0	6 15	8 35
	Kidlington	arr.	7 10	8 10	11 10	3 10	6 25	8 45

The June 1890 Working Timetable.

One of the earliest known photographs of Blenheim & Woodstock station, this 19th century scene was probably taken to show No. 1473's newly applied nameplates in the early months of 1896. The single slip beneath the locomotive was removed around 1898.
Mrs. R. Giraud

shed, and that the tiny coaling stage at Blenheim & Woodstock (which had in any case been removed by 1899) was used only for 'topping-up' purposes.

The paucity of through workings was just one symptom of an organisational flaw that had revealed itself as early as July 1890. The Woodstock Railway Company had no large body of supporters willing to put themselves forward as directors — indeed, the only significant local supporter was the Duke of Marlborough and he displayed little interest in the new railway. This was doubly unfortunate in so far as the Woodstock Railway's operating agreement placed responsibility for staffing and other matters in *local* hands; however, the Woodstock company was unwilling to provide station staff, and on 8th July 1890 the Company Secretary was instructed to write to Paddington with a request for assistance. The Great Western agreed that they would lend such staff 'as may be necessary for the working and services of the Woodstock Company', and a compromise arrangement was soon arranged whereby the local company paid the GWR for the 'borrowed' staff. The Great Western employees involved were 'deemed to be the staff of the Woodstock Company' — but this was of course an accountant's technicality.

A similar arrangement was requested when Lucas & Aird's contract for permanent way maintenance expired in May 1891. Needless to say, the Woodstock Railway had no wish to maintain its own track, and the Secretary was again instructed to contact Paddington, asking if the GWR would undertake all PW maintenance. The matter was discussed by the Great Western Board on 14th May, but having learned that the cost of maintaining the line on the renewal principle would be £580 a year (or if a lower standard was acceptable, £460 a year), the GW directors declined to help. Signals and telegraph presented a further problem, but on 4th June 1891 the Woodstock Railway Board authorised Mr Woods to arrange a contract with Mr Spagnolleti (the GWR's signalling expert) and Messrs Saxby & Farmer 'for maintenance of the telegraphs and signals for a year'.

Locomotives & Rolling Stock in the 1890s

The original branch timetable, with its basic service of five trains each way, was worked by a single locomotive and train set; the engine was sub-shedded at Blenheim & Woodstock, and was usually a '517' class tank engine. Dating from the mid-1860s, these locomotives had been designed by George Armstrong and built at Wolverhampton; when first introduced they had 15 in × 24 in cylinders and carried their water in saddle tanks. The initial batch had very short coupled wheelbases which gave them a rather ungainly appearance — though they were nevertheless highly efficient machines with a commendably small coal consumption. From 1870 the engines were rebuilt as side tanks with an extended wheelbase and as such they became the first members of the '517' class — a numerous class which remained in production until 1895 and was eventually to be found all over the GWR system.

The regular Woodstock branch engine was No 1473 — one of the later '517's — and by March 1896 this locomotive had been given the romantic name *Fair Rosamund* in commemoration of Rosamund Clifford (who was then enjoying something of a revival in the pages of local guide books). No 1473's nameplates were fixed to her side tanks immediately above the brass number plates; it is possible that this naming was an unofficial innovation, but the idea was immensely popular and No 1473 carried her distinctive nameplates for over forty years. In time the Woodstock branch trains became known as 'Rosie' and this affectionate sobriquet remained in common use long after the original *Fair Rosamund* had been broken up. It remains a matter of conjecture why No 1473 was named, but the likeliest explanation is that for some reason VIP specials were hauled to Woodstock by the regular branch tank engine. It made sense, therefore, to distinguish the branch engine in some way in order that the VIPs concerned would not feel insulted by the appearance of an otherwise ordinary locomotive at the head of their train.

Little is known for sure about the coaching stock used at the time of opening, but photographic evidence suggests that the regular formation included one or two Dean clerestories. Six-wheeled coaches could also have been used, and it is possible that some heavily-used services were composed of both eight-wheeled and short wheelbase six-wheeled stock. In this context it is worth remembering that the 1890 Act had specified 'one long composite carriage . . . and one third class carriage', which suggests a formation of 1 bogie vehicle plus one six-wheeler.

As mentioned in Chapter One, there may have been an overtly political motive behind the Duke of Marlborough's desire to build a railway to Blenheim. As we have seen, the station at Woodstock was well-equipped to handle special excursions, and such trains ran quite often during the 1890s when various political or quasi-political organisations chose Blenheim Palace as a venue for meetings or rallies. Many of these functions were associated with the Conservative Party while others were of purely local importance, such as flower displays, cricket matches or agricultural shows.

Among the more unusual events held at Blenheim was a great review of firemen, which took place in July 1895. Local brigades presumably came by road, but those from further afield travelled by train in order to take part in a military-style procession — the road from the station to the park being specially decorated for their benefit.

In addition to incoming excursions there were occasional specials *from* the station and on Thursday, 4th July 1895 there was a seaside excursion from Woodstock to Portsmouth. (Although there was nothing to compare with the annual migrations from Leeds to Morecambe, or from Nottingham to Skegness, the facts of geography made Portsmouth a favourite seaside destination for Oxfordshire people.)

Lord Randolph's Funeral

These events brought much extra traffic to the line, but sadly the Eighth Duke of Marlborough did not survive really long enough to see his railway playing its part in local life, for he died suddenly in 1892 at the early age of forty-eight. Even more tragic was the slow demise of Lord Randolph Churchill, whose meteoric rise had thrust Blenheim into the forefront of national life. The victim of an unfortunate disease, his behaviour had become increasingly erratic, and, having quarrelled with most of his colleagues, Randolph resigned from public office in 1887. His career in ruins, this brilliant politician deteriorated slowly throughout the early 1890s, and as paralysis approached he suffered from facial twitches, slurred speech and terrifying delusions; in June 1894 he was sent on a world cruise — though he was by this time virtually insane. He finally died in London on Thursday, 24th January 1895, the unmentionable illness having reached his brain. On Monday the 28th, Lord Randolph's body was brought back to Woodstock by train for burial at nearby Bladon.

It may be, that in the course of an after-dinner discussion with his brother, Lord Randolph had raised the subject of a privately-financed rail link, and so initiated the Woodstock Railway project. If this was indeed the case, it was sad, but entirely appropriate, that the dead politician should have returned home to Woodstock by train, and in the course of a very full and entirely sympathetic obituary (which tactfully did not inquire into the cause of death) the *Oxfordshire Weekly News* reported his final journey as follows:–

> 'The remains of the late Lord Randolph Churchill were on Monday removed from Grosvenor Square to Paddington Station for conveyance to Bladon Church, near Woodstock, where the interment took place . . . At Paddington the large crowd which had gathered had to be regulated by a force of police and the departure platform was kept private except to the friends . . . the large bridges spanning the station, and other platforms were densely packed with persons anxious to catch a sight of the coffin. The special train conveying the coffin and mourners to Woodstock left the station at 10 o'clock, all persons present respectfully uncovering. At Twyford, Goring and other intermediate stations small groups made a similar display of feeling. At Oxford there was a brief stoppage and the Bishop (Dr Stubbs) and his chaplain (Dr Yule) joined the train. Woodstock was reached a few minutes before twelve. Upon the platform and at the entrance were the Mayor (Mr W.P. Clarke) and members of the Corporation with craped mace, and the Woodstock & Blenheim Fire Brigades, the local A.O.F. of which Lord Randolph was formerly an honorary member; the Blenheim estate tenantry, and the Conservative Association. Large numbers of townspeople thronged the approaches, mourning being everywhere observable. The principal places of business were closed, and blinds were generally drawn at private residences. Within Woodstock Church, where the first part of the burial service was impressively rendered, there was a large congregation.'

More Special Workings

Although the people of Woodstock had not been told the precise nature of Lord Randolph's illness, the loss of two prominent local personalities in less than three years cast a cloud over the little town, and when in the following year the

Fair Rosamund stands in Woodstock station at the head of the Royal Train which conveyed HRH the Prince of Wales to Blenheim on 23rd November 1896; the stars and stripes was possibly a leftover from the Duke's wedding special of the previous March! The people in front of the engine appear to be local railwaymen, Blenheim Estate staff, and local dignitaries. Station master Ashford is fourth from the right.

Ninth Duke brought his American bride back to Blenheim the townsfolk welcomed an opportunity to rejoice. Indeed, the resulting festivities were without precedent and far outshone the events that had accompanied the line's rather restrained Opening Day.

Like his father and his Uncle Randolph, the Ninth Duke had seen the financial advantages accruing to British aristocrats who married American heiresses, and in 1895 he himself married Miss Consuelo Vanderbilt (knowing that the Duke did not love her, Consuelo had gone to the altar in tears). The unhappy couple travelled from Paddington to Woodstock on 31st March 1896, leaving London at 1.30 pm and arriving in Oxford at 2.48 pm. It seems that the Duke and Duchess were conveyed in a special saloon carriage and the *Oxford Times*' report which appeared on the following Saturday stated that 'when the Birkenhead portion of the express had been despatched, the Woodstock branch engine *Fair Rosamund*, decorated with evergreens and the Stars and Stripes, and bearing the words WELCOME HOME upon the front, was backed on to the saloon, and amid hearty cheers of the spectators who crowded the station and a *feu de joie* of detonators placed on the rails over which it passed, the train left at three o'clock for Blenheim'. The special halted at Kidlington, where the station had been specially decorated by station master William Cooke, the gas lamps being hidden by floral decorations, pot plants and flowers. Winifred Cooke, the station master's daughter, presented the Duchess with a bouquet of roses, and then the train resumed its journey, passing beneath the word WELCOME which spanned the bridge arch in red Japonica.

'As the train sped onwards', continued the *Times*, 'little knots of spectators clustered around the farmhouses, and the flags that caught the eye from time to time in the trees and meadows adjacent to the railway reminded the Duchess that she was at last nearing home'. Meanwhile, chosen guests had assembled on the platform at Woodstock, while thousands more milled about outside the station. 'At 3.13 pm the ringing of a bell in the Station Master's office indicated that the train had left Kidlington, and five minutes later it steamed into the station amidst cheers from the National School children massed on the opposite platform.' Emerging from their train, the Duke and Duchess walked along the platform to the booking hall, which was 'tastefully furnished with palms, arum lilies and other choice pot plants'. Leaving the station, the Duke raised his hat to the cheering crowds and then continued through Woodstock to the Town Hall where various celebrations had been arranged. Finally, the recently-married couple rode in triumph to Blenheim Palace and the great day ended with a spectacular firework display; truly, Woodstock had laid on a 'right royal welcome'.

Other important events held at Blenheim in 1896 included a drill session for the Yeomanry on 18th April and a large Conservative & Unionist Rally on Saturday, 5th September; this last-named event was attended by 2000 party delegates, most of whom would have reached Woodstock by train (there was no other way to travel in those days!). In addition the palace grounds provided an attractive venue for the usual round of cricket matches and agricultural events, and finally, towards the end of the year, HRH the Prince of Wales travelled to Blenheim and the Woodstock branch played host to the royal train.

A Royal Visit

Built as a state palace in celebration of a national victory, Blenheim was well-suited to welcome and entertain royal guests and on Monday, 23rd November, it was able to do so for the first time in over twenty years. Curiously, the welcome given to Prince Edward was noticeably restrained when compared to the euphoria which had greeted the Duke's recent homecoming, and one can only conclude that the citizens of Woodstock were becoming tired of such grand occasions (the damp November weather may also have been a factor). Nevertheless, Woodstock was once again decorated for an honoured visitor, with flags, floral arches, and hundreds of fairy lights strung out picturesquely between the station and the town hall. The station was specially prepared, and extensive canvas screens led from its carpeted platform to the booking hall — which was turned into a reception area complete with potted palms and other embellishments. Kidlington, too, was specially decorated (presumably with floral decorations left over from the previous March).

The royal train left Paddington at 4.55 pm and ran non-stop to Kidlington; the formation on this occasion included a six-wheeled brake van, the royal saloon, two other saloons and an eight-wheel bogie brake vehicle. On arrival at Kidlington the main line engine was detached and replaced by *Fair Rosamund*, which then hauled the royal train for the final 3¾ miles to Woodstock. Arrival was at 6.39 pm, one minute ahead of schedule. The *Oxford Times* reporter noted that *Fair Rosamund* had been 'embellished with a huge wreath of fir leaves, forming a setting for the word WELCOME, while numerous small flags were affixed in prominent positions'. Reports of the visit make no mention of the customary pilot engine which was usually run ahead of every royal special; perhaps this precaution was deemed unnecessary on the short journey between Kidlington and Woodstock?

The Prince stayed at Blenheim for several days and then returned to his home at Sandringham via Oxford and the L & NWR; the eight-mile journey to Oxford station was made by road, with an escort of mounted Yeomanry. (Although the cheering crowds did not know it, royal visits to Blenheim were rare because Randolph had foolishly involved the Prince of Wales in a scandal involving his brother George, a duel, and a royal mistress.)

The End of Local Control

Having, largely through their own efforts, striven to build the railway, the Churchills had no particular desire to permanently control it. As far as they were concerned, the Great Western was doing a good job in actually running the trains — and in any case the Eighth Duke, who had built the Woodstock Railway, was now dead. Moreover, the line was not, by any stretch of the imagination, a financial success, and, although it was highly valued as an amenity, the Ninth Duke could hardly be expected to pay for such a public service out of his own pocket.

In truth, the railway was losing money, and this had been clear since March 1893 when the local company had told the GWR that it was no longer in a position to make further payments and would have to end the existing working agreement. This may have been merely a ploy to exact better terms from the Great Western, but if so the gambit was unsuccessful. The Great Western General Manager met the Woodstock Railway's representatives on 22nd April 1893 and was told that the receipts had fallen considerably short of the amount payable to the GWR under the terms of the operating agreement. Under these circumstances the Woodstock directors asked if the Great Western would consider purchasing the entire line for £20,000 with no charge being made for the land. Alternatively, it was suggested that the Great Western might work the branch as a tramway with consequent savings in fuel and staffing costs. If neither of these courses of action was successful, threatened the Woodstock directors, 'the line would have to be closed'.

The tramway idea was an interesting concept which may well have been inspired by the opening of the neighbouring Shipston-on-Stour 'Steam Tramway' by the GWR on 1st July 1889 (local papers such as the *Oxford Times* had covered the Shipston line in considerable detail, and the Woodstock directors would certainly have been aware of this early attempt at 'basic railway' operation). Sadly, the Great Western failed to respond to this approach, and instead the company offered to suspend the operating agreement for a period 'say of ten years' during which time they would 'raise no objection to the line being worked as a tramway, subject however to the payment . . . of £150 per annum'. This suggestion was probably made as a counter move by the GWR, and the Great Western directors must surely have known that their counterparts on the Woodstock Railway Board were unwilling or unable to run the railway themselves. Neither would the GWR have been particularly bothered if the line was closed — in that case they would not have to operate its unremunerative services. Indeed, there was little to indicate that the Great Western had any interest in the Woodstock Railway whatsoever — though if its purchase price came down they would no doubt be willing to absorb the line.

The next move came from Charles Lucas who, having taken a large number of shares in the company, was still intimately connected with the railway. On 26th October 1893 the Great Western directors were told that:–

> 'Mr Lucas, who is a large shareholder in the Woodstock Company, has recently had an interview with the Chairman with respect to the undertaking and . . . Mr J. Hargrove of the firm of Messrs Hargrove & Co. Solicitors, acting on behalf of the Woodstock Company, had interviewed with the General Manager on the same subject'.

Lucas (who may have hoped that the 'friendly approach' would work) suggested that the line might be sold at the low price of £10,000, but, after brief consideration of this generous offer, the Great Western Board declined to purchase the branch.

Thwarted in their attempts to divest themselves of the Woodstock Railway, John Aird, Charles Lucas and the Duke of Marlborough opened a new offensive in the autumn of 1893 when they warned the unhelpful GWR Board that they had considered depositing a Bill for the purpose of putting an end to the existing operating agreement '*and granting the Woodstock Railway Co. compulsorily running powers over the GWR from Kidlington into Oxford*'. The threat of such a Bill was enough to make the Great Western take a more sympathetic interest in the Woodstock Railway's problems, and in November 1893 the GWR General Manager was instructed to write to the Woodstock Company, stating that if the latter failed to fulfil its obligations under the working agreement, the GWR, in order to prevent 'inconvenience to the public', would be prepared to make up any deficiencies incurred by the Woodstock Railway under the agreement. This course of action would 'afford an opportunity for considering any arrangement as to the future working of the undertaking'. The Great Western had in effect given in to the Woodstock Railway, and for the next few months the local company was content to retain control of the railway.

There were renewed sale negotiations with the Great Western in 1896, when, at a meeting arranged between John Aird, the Duke, and the GWR General Manager, the Woodstock representatives asked if the GWR would be willing to pay £25,000 for the entire undertaking. The Great Western again declined, but the larger company was interested enough to make an offer of £10,000. A further meeting took place towards the end of the year, and on this occasion John Aird was able to extract a much better offer of £15,000 from the Great Western.

The proposed purchase of the Woodstock Railway was discussed by the GWR Board on 8th October 1896, and the Great Western directors authorised the acquisition of the branch under the following terms:–

> 'The sum of £15,000, viz £5,000 in cash for the . . . Debenture Stock of the Woodstock Co, and £10,000 in cash in respect of the Ordinary shares, the debt due from the Woodstock Co . . . being cancelled'.

The final meeting of the Woodstock Railway Company was held in Lucas & Aird's offices at 37 Great George Street, Westminster, those present being John Aird MP, John Aird Junior, John W. Palmer, and other representatives of the company. The Great Western's latest terms were fully accepted, and it was 'resolved that Mr William Fountain Woods of 37 Great George Street Westminster, the secretary of the Company, be . . . appointed the liquidator'.

The winding-up process was surprisingly complex and involved a further Act of Parliament which went through both houses in 1897; however, the Woodstock Railway was finally sold to the Great Western on 1st July 1897, when the necessary Act was obtained. The GWR had been making similar acquisitions for several years as part of a 'tidying up' operation in which local companies were brought into the fold. In most cases these locally-owned lines had been worked by the Great Western from their inception, and the effect of such take-overs was usually minimal; local directors invariably felt that a financial load had been taken from their shoulders, while ordinary travellers would probably have been blissfully unaware that a change had taken place!

Some Effects of the Railway

The opening of the Woodstock branch made little difference to life in the area and there were no significant changes, either in local transport or in the town's economy. It is true that townsfolk could now travel by train to Oxford for shopping and other purposes, but the new railway did not totally replace the old carrier services and, on the contrary, perusal of successive editions of *Kelly's Directory* suggests that road transport services actually increased after 1890. Moreover, as carriers' carts were cheaper than the trains (and served a wider range of destinations), the suspicion must be that many ordinary countryfolk preferred to travel by this inexpensive and unhurried means. Waterways, too, played an important part in local transport long after 1890, and when, in 1905, the Oxford Portland Cement Company established an important works in the area, the new industry relied entirely upon the supposedly-obsolete Oxford Canal.

Neither did a direct rail link lead to mechanisation of the gloving industry; J & R Pullman & Sons of Godalming built a new factory beside the station in 1889, and it was stated that this new works was able to turn out over 1,200 pairs of gloves a week. For a time the company carried out some of its preliminary work at Woodstock, but after a few years this 'industrial' stage of glove production was concentrated in Pullman's home base at Godalming, and Woodstock was left with little more than a 'craft workshop'. In later years one or two other glove manufacturers opened similar workshops, but these relied entirely on treadle-operated sewing machines and the Woodstock premises were 'factories' in name only. The local gloving trade remained a small-scale craft industry, organised predominantly along domestic lines, and as such it did not give rise to any bulk freight traffic, though the railway was used to bring in raw skins and send out small hampers of completed gloves.

Opened in 1890, the Woodstock Railway arrived too late to materially improve the town, and its main purpose must be seen as an adjunct to the political and social life of nearby Blenheim Palace. George Behrend has claimed that 'Blenheim & Woodstock' was a typically Great Western name, placing a palace first and a centre of population second. In plebeian Britain today, he suggests, such a station would be called Woodstock for Blenheim. While this may be true, the fact remains that Woodstock's railway was built by a landed magnate, and given the circumstances surrounding Blenheim's role in late Victorian politics it must be admitted that the name *Blenheim* & Woodstock was entirely appropriate! (There was in November 1902 a suggestion that the station should be renamed, but — significantly — this idea was never implemented and most Woodstock residents were content to let the palace take symbolic precedence.)

A Note on Tickets and Uniforms

The Woodstock Railway minute book contains an intriguingly brief reference to the provision of uniforms, but, although Mr Woods was instructed to 'arrange uniforms', there is no further reference to this subject and one must assume that Woodstock Railway staff wore ordinary GWR issue jackets, trousers and waistcoats. However, Blenheim estate staff *did* wear a distinctive dark green uniform with two rows of shiny buttons, and it would have been logical for at least some of their counterparts at the station to sport crested Churchill buttons (or perhaps cap badges). There is, unfortunately, no way of knowing if Mr Lofting or any of the other 'borrowed' GWR staff wore such additions to their normal uniforms, but no such mystery surrounds the tickets issued at Blenheim & Woodstock prior to 1897, which were Edmondson cards bearing the heading 'Woodstock Railway Co'. The tickets were in other respects standard Great Western issues conforming to the usual late Victorian colour codes for first, second, third, excursion, market, dogs and other bookings.

(No 240.)

GREAT WESTERN RAILWAY.

(For the use of the Company's Servants only.)

NOTICE OF

SPECIAL TRAIN

FROM

WINDSOR

TO

BLENHEIM

AND BACK,

ON

Friday, November 24th, 1899.

TIME TABLE.

FORWARD JOURNEY.	pass arr. P.M.	dep. NOON	RETURN JOURNEY.	pass arr. P.M.	dep. P.M.
WINDSOR	—	12 0	**BLENHEIM**	Time of return uncertain. Special will probably leave **Blenheim about 3.30 p.m.** Station Masters at all Stations must be on the look out for telegraphic advice and must endeavour to keep a clear road for the Special.	
Slough West Curve **A**	**ML** 12	6	Kidlington		
Maidenhead	12	12	Oxford (Middle Road)		
Reading	12	24	Didcot East Junction		
Didcot East Junction	12	43	Reading		
Oxford (Middle Road)	12	56	Maidenhead		
Kidlington ... **B**	1 4	1 7	Slough West Curve ...		
BLENHEIM	**1 15**	—	**WINDSOR**		

A To precede the 11.45 a.m. Express from Paddington from Slough.

B A Separate Engine to be provided at Kidlington on Down journey to enable Train Engine to be detached there and run to Oxford to turn. Train Engine to return to Blenheim in good time to work the Special Train through from there to Windsor.

A working notice issued prior to the visit of Kaiser Wilhelm of Germany to Blenheim in 1899.

CHAPTER FOUR

A GREAT WESTERN BRANCH LINE (1897–1947)

IN physical terms the GWR made various small changes to the track layout at Woodstock, and these alterations (which may have started as early as 1897) eliminated the complex piece of trackwork at the western end of the terminus. The single slip was removed and the main goods siding was partially slewed onto a new alignment; the western extremity of this siding then became a short dead-end spur capable of holding two bogie vehicles. Meanwhile, the lengthy run-round loop was given an intermediate crossover (presumably to allow more siding capacity). When the end of the loop line was occupied by wagons or spare coaches branch locomotives could still run round, but the full 800 ft loop was still available for long mixed trains, excursions or VIP specials, of which there were a considerable number during the early 1900s. The platform was also lengthened, apparently entailing the removal of the engine shed spur to a new position somewhat further to the east, and the corrugated-iron engine shed was moved a few feet to facilitate these alterations.

The remodelling of Blenheim & Woodstock station took several months to complete, but the bulk of the work was carried out between March and October 1899. There is some evidence of indecision on the part of the GWR engineering department, with indications that a bay platform was originally considered and then rejected. Despite this apparent vacillation, the Great Western wrote to the Board of Trade on 10th May 1899, enclosing a 'plan of two siding connections' which it was proposed to lay at the terminus, and asking if the new works could be 'brought into use as and when required on the understanding that it is submitted for inspection when complete'. The GWR letter explained that it was proposed to hold an agricultural show at Blenheim & Woodstock in the near future, and asked if, in these circumstances, 'the connections in question' could be brought 'into use on Monday next'.

It is conceivable that the works referred to were temporary connections designed to increase siding capacity for the duration of the show. Significantly the plan sent to the Board of Trade showed a triple-armed home signal with one bracket controlling entry to a new siding on the down side, which may in fact have been a bay. If this was indeed the case, the bay must have been lifted a few weeks later during the course of continuing engineering work at the station, and on 18th October 1899 the company sent a further letter to the Board of Trade, indicating that the remodelling was complete and asking when the new layout could be inspected; the BOT replied that Colonel Yorke would inspect the terminus, and on 18th December he reported as follows:–

> 'I have the honour to report for the information of the Board of Trade that in compliance with the instructions contained in your memorandum of the 19th October, I have inspected the two new connections on the single line at Blenheim & Woodstock station on the Great Western Railway. The points and signals are worked from the existing signal box which contains 18 levers, all in use, and correctly interlocked.
>
> I can recommend the BOT to sanction the use of these works.
>
> I am, etc., etc., H.A. Yorke, RE'

A further innovation, put into effect by the GWR after 1897, concerned the line's signalling. Hitherto the single line between Kidlington and Woodstock had been worked by train staff and ticket which allowed successive trains to follow each other down the branch once their drivers had received written authorisation. Although this system had worked safely, the Great Western installed electrically interlocked train staff equipment in Woodstock and Kidlington signal boxes, thereby reducing the risk of 'human error'.

As a result of these improvements signalling at Blenheim & Woodstock became relatively complex, and by 1899 the terminus was equipped with an up starter, an up advanced starter, and (for a short time at least) an up loop starter for goods traffic. In the opposite direction, signals provided included a down distant, and a down home with two subsidiary siding arms. The signals themselves were, apparently, ordinary GWR square-posted semaphores.

The most complex feature of the branch's signalling at this time was undoubtedly the system at Kidlington which allowed main line trains to occupy the single line. This system was installed in 1907, and in his inspection report dated 19th August, Colonel Yorke described it as follows:–

> 'There is an arrangement here whereby the facing points leading from the down main to the branch are locked by a key which is electrically controlled by the electric staffing of the single line branch, the control being such that the key cannot be taken out and points leading to the branch cannot be moved so long as any of the train staffs are out, and, conversely, when the key is out of the instrument no staff can be released at either end of the single line. The object of this arrangement is that it is occasionally required to 'refuge' a down goods train on the single line branch in order to clear the road for a through train, and it is required to ensure that no train shall be on the branch line when this is done.'

An Orange Demonstration

The Woodstock Railway continued to play what might be loosely termed a 'political' role throughout the Edwardian period, with fêtes, party rallies and similar functions bringing extra traffic and occasionally necessitating special trains. The greatest of these rallies took place on Saturday, 27th July 1912 when, at a time when Northern Ireland was preparing to resist Home Rule by force of arms, large numbers of Unionists converged on Blenheim Palace to take part in a controversial Anti-Home Rule rally.

The choice of Blenheim as the venue for this event was itself highly symbolic, for in an earlier speech (at Belfast in 1886) the late Lord Randolph Churchill had thrilled his Irish audience with the words ULSTER WILL FIGHT AND ULSTER WILL BE RIGHT — and at a time when Asquith's Liberal government was preparing to force the Protestant north-eastern counties of Ireland to accept a Catholic-dominated Home Rule Parliament, the Orangemen of Belfast had not forgotten Randolph's forthright message! In fact the United Kingdom of Great Britain '& Ireland' was, in that summer of 1912, dangerously close to civil war and in these grave and unhappy circumstances all eyes were focused on Blenheim.

An aerial view of Blenheim & Woodstock station, showing its relation to Woodstock and Blenheim Palace. Oxford Road can be seen running diagonally across the photograph from top left to bottom right, while High Street diverges at an angle to the right. The Church of England school is visible beside the station, and, a little further south, Hensington Gate gives access to Blenheim Park. Note how the long, thin, medieval burgage plots have dictated the shape of the station.

Aerofilms

A postcard view of the French garden at Blenheim – this Edwardian scene shows merely a fragment of the huge palace and conveys little of the grandeur of Vanburgh's heroic design. (It is thought that this card was sent by a newly appointed chamber maid to her friends at home.)

Author's Collection

Unionist Party Demonstration.

BLENHEIM

(BY INVITATION OF THE DUKE OF MARLBOROUGH)

SATURDAY, 27TH JULY, 1912

ADMIT BEARER TO

MASS MEETING

TO BE HELD IN

THE COURT YARD, NORTH FRONT, BLENHEIM PALACE.

SPEAKERS:

THE RIGHT HON. A. BONAR LAW, M.P.

THE RIGHT HON. SIR EDWARD H. CARSON, K.C., M.P.

THE RIGHT HON. F. E. SMITH, K.C., M.P.

CHAIR TAKEN AT 2.30 P.M.

This Ticket admits to the MASS MEETING ONLY. P.T.O.

An interesting (and probably extremely rare) 'invitation' to the famous July 1912 Anti-Home Rule Rally. Sir Edward Carson (a Dublin lawyer and close friend of Lady Randolph) was the champion of Irish Protestantism, in the way that Ian Paisley is today. *Trevor Cooper*

It had been expected that from 3000 to 3500 Unionists would turn up to hear Sir Edward Carson, Bonar Law and other 'Orange' leaders vociferously denounce treacherous Liberal politicians and their attempts to destroy the United Kingdom by giving Home Rule to the 32 counties of Ireland. In the event, up to 20,000 people travelled by train to Handborough and Woodstock stations — many arriving in no less than four excursions from Paddington; a fifth GWR special ran from Shrewsbury, while the Great Central provided three workings from the North and Midlands. There was also a Great Eastern special from the Norwich area, and, in addition to these long distance trains, the normal branch service was augmented by many extra workings between Oxford and Woodstock.

Bonar Law and the other MPs arrived at 12.30 pm and were welcomed on the platform at Woodstock by the Duke of Marlborough; the official party then proceeded from the station to the palace. Huge crowds already thronged the narrow streets of Woodstock, and the Anti-Home Rule MPs were cheered time and time again as they progressed through the town. In his speech, Bonar Law expressed the full support of his party for whatever action Irish loyalists might take in their fight to remain full British citizens; they would, he believed, be supported by 'the overwhelming majority of the British people'. In spite of this barely-concealed appeal to men of violence, the great rally ended peacefully, and thousands of Unionists enjoyed a picnic in the park before returning to their homes in the late afternoon.

Meanwhile, Prince Edward's 1896 visit to Blenheim had been taken as a sure sign that the Churchills were back in royal favour, and by the early 1900s 'Society' was flocking to Blenheim on a scale that only a few years before would have been unimaginable. With motoring still in its infancy, most of Blenheim's rich and famous guests arrived by train — among them Kaiser Wilhelm II and his son the Crown Prince of Germany.

Obviously, the arrival of a foreign head of state was treated as a ceremonial occasion, and the station would be decorated accordingly. In terms of traffic, however, a ball or a shooting party was equally important; having married the Vanderbilt millions, the Duke of Marlborough could afford to entertain on a lavish scale and his many house guests would arrive with scores of servants and mountains of luggage. The Duke and Duchess invariably met their guests on the station platform, and accompanied them to the palace in convoys of horse-drawn carriages. Station staff became used to the sight of famous celebrities *en route* to or from the nearby palace — some of the Duke's house guests were generous tippers!

All of the Churchills became well-known at the station, but older people are most likely to remember 'The Yankee Ladies' — Lady Randolph and Consuelo, Duchess of Marlborough. Lady Randolph Churchill (Winston Churchill's mother) was one of the most beautiful women of her age; her ancestors had been French Huguenots, but it was rumoured (correctly) that her striking dark hair was evidence of Red Indian blood. It was, perhaps, hardly surprising that she formed many romantic attachments — but few Woodstock residents could have guessed that one of her close acquaintances was Edward, the Prince of Wales. Consuelo, Duchess of Marlborough, was less of a beauty, but she won the hearts of all in Woodstock. As mentioned earlier, the Ninth Duke had married her for money — and as good as told her so. On arrival in England in March 1896, the Duke's mother had asked bluntly if she was 'in the family way'. The reply being negative, her mother-in-law told her that her first duty was to have children — one of whom would *have* to be a boy, otherwise *'that little upstart Winston'* would become the next Duke!

Consuelo's appearance was somewhat unusual; a combination of upturned nose, high cheekbones and curiously-arched eyebrows gave her a quizzical, slightly comic face, and although not in any way ugly, she lacked the classic beauty of Lady Randolph. Neither did she fit easily into Edwardian upper class society; at King Edward's coronation, for instance, she alone turned up adorned with jewels and finery — an incongruous figure when most of the other ladies were wearing plain black (the Duke had probably not told her what the other ladies would be wearing at this state occasion). It is clear from her own memoirs that the new Duchess felt lonely and ill-at-ease amid the architectural splendours of Blenheim, and perhaps for this reason she took a great interest in the day-to-day lives of ordinary people. George Franklin remembered that she would individually thank porters and other station staff for carrying luggage or opening doors when she travelled by train, while others recalled that she would frequently distribute tins of food to the poor and needy. Sadly, the Ninth Duke eventually divorced Consuelo, and, having acquired through marriage a considerable dowry, he then married Gladys Deacon of Boston. Consuelo, meanwhile, lived to a ripe old age and in 1964 *she* was buried in the family plot at Bladon, achieving, in death, lasting recognition as the 'true' Ninth Duchess of Marlborough.

Winston Churchill had been a frequent visitor to the Palace, and he is remembered locally as a precocious, red-headed child; one day he was out riding, and rather than say 'excuse me' to a village girl who had innocently blocked his path, he threatened to get down from his horse and whip her out of the way. 'If you do that', she answered, 'I'll tan your hide, and what is more *I'll tell your grandma*'; understandably alarmed at this mention of his formidable grandmother (the Seventh Duchess), young Winston trotted back to the palace.

An Edwardian view looking eastwards, over the buffers at Woodstock, with the signal box and engine shed visible in the background. Although Woodstock's gardens were extremely well tended by Ashford and his staff, they were usually overshadowed by the prize-winning displays at Kidlington. *Mrs. R. Giraud*

In August 1906 the Woodstock Corps of the St. John Ambulance Brigade paraded and marched to Blenheim Palace to receive an award at the hands of the Duchess of Marlborough; among those receiving presentation were members of the station staff, including Thomas Ashford (left) and Messrs. Hunt, Godman, Peare, Hine and Bryant. Here the ambulancemen post self-consciously with their stretcher in front of *Fair Rosamund* which has now lost her small backplate. *Mrs. R. Giraud*

Another view of station master Ashford (seated) and his ambulancemen at the time of their 1906 parade. *Mrs. R. Giraud*

A general view of Blenheim & Woodstock station at the turn of the century. Although an original of this photograph has not yet been traced, the engine shed and signal cabin can nevertheless be glimpsed in the distance; station master Thomas Ashford and his entire staff are standing on the platform. Study of the photograph reveals the platform extension, presumably carried out in connection with the agricultural show held at Blenheim in May 1899. *Great Western Magazine*

Other stories recall the future Prime Minister hitching lifts on the back of farm wagons and carriers' carts, and sitting on the back with his feet dangling over the tailboard! (These incidents are however more likely to have taken place in the 1880s *before* the railway was open — though Winston is known to have spent the Christmas of 1893 with 'Grandma Marlborough' at Blenheim.)

Locomotives and train services in the Edwardian Period

No 1473 *Fair Rosamund* remained the regular Woodstock branch engine, helped out on occasions (e.g. during boiler washouts, etc.) by other '517' Class 0–4–2Ts. It is possible that 'Metro' 2–4–0Ts or other small tank engines also appeared from time to time, but photographic evidence, incidental references and personal recollections all suggest that No 1473 was the Woodstock branch engine *par excellence* until her eventual withdrawal in 1935. In time, this engine underwent many rebuilds and appeared in several guises. When first built, she had a round-topped firebox, half cab and a low bunker, together with a characteristic Great Western copper chimney cap and brass boiler fittings; the full GW lined green livery was carried. By 1910 *Fair Rosamund* had acquired new side tanks and an enlarged coal bunker, and ten years later a flat-topped Belpaire firebox had replaced the original rounded version. In the final ten years of her life *Fair Rosamund* carried a full cab of comparatively modern appearance, and sported a plain green livery with few copper or brass adornments; by 1930 her brass GW numberplates had been moved from the centre to the rear of her side tanks to make room for large GREAT WESTERN transfers — hitherto the little engine had carried no indication of ownership. On a footnote, *Fair Rosamund* was never given outside bearings to her trailing wheels, though sister engine No 1159 received this modification.

The Edwardian period was the heyday of the steam railmotor car and by 1908 the Great Western had acquired 99 of these vehicles together with 101 power units. Each vehicle consisted of a large saloon coach with a powered bogie at one end and an ordinary coach bogie at the other — the power bogies being in effect tiny 0–4–0 locomotives with vertical boilers and 12 in × 16 in inside cylinders; their coupled wheelbase was 8 ft. The cars could be driven from either end and were, in many ways, the forerunners of all later single and multiple unit vehicles. The earliest examples had vertical matchboard sides with no 'tumblehome', but from No 29 onwards the cars followed the profiles of ordinary Great Western coaches.

Timetables show that steam railmotors worked some off-peak Woodstock services during the early 1900s, and one photograph has come to light showing a railmotor at

Fair Rosamund posed in front of Blenheim & Woodstock signal cabin. Bill Pomeroy, the regular Woodstock driver, is standing with his hand on the cab rail. *Miss F. Budd*

Woodstock. The use of such vehicles was popular with regular travellers; the large all-round windows provided excellent views of the surrounding countryside, and in service it seems that the Great Western cars were surprisingly quiet, emitting a barely-audible 'phut phut phut' sound. At speed, their small wheels contributed to a slightly jerky motion, but this was not really apparent at the rear of the cars — in any case the overall level of vibration felt by travellers was much less than that endured by modern DMU passengers. In 1908, the 1.55 pm down service from Oxford to Woodstock and the 2.52 pm return working was worked by a railmotor; both of these services called at Wolvercot Halt — a railmotor platform situated midway between Oxford and Kidlington and opened on 1st February 1908.

A steam railmotor in Blenheim & Woodstock station, probably c.1908. *Mrs. R. Giraud*

The Great Western's steam railmotors worked successfully for several years, but ultimately the company realised that greater flexibility could be achieved by the use of locomotives and driving trailers, and many former railmotors were subsequently converted for use as unpowered trailers. These new combinations eventually appeared on the Woodstock branch, and in time the line was worked exclusively by push-pull or 'auto-trains'. In the early 1900s, however, the line was still worked, in the main, by conventional locomotives and coaches, the engine running round its train at Woodstock, Oxford or Kidlington.

The basic weekday service consisted, in the early 1900s, of four passenger trains and two mixed workings each way, but in 1908 an improved service was introduced and the July 1908 working timetable shows eight workings each way. Operations began at 7.53 am with an early morning train from Woodstock to Kidlington which returned at 8.20 am as a 'mixed' working from Kidington to Woodstock. The branch locomotive then made two more return trips before arriving back in Woodstock with another 'mixed' working at 1.03 pm. The next three hours were obviously a slack period, and, while the branch engine carried out any shunting duties that might be required at Woodstock, the passenger service was taken over by an Oxford-based steam railmotor. Having completed its shunting, the locomotive worked a 'mixed' to Kidlington and returned with the 3.48 passenger working from Kidlington to Woodstock. The remainder of the timetable consisted of three more return workings to Oxford or Kidlington, including a 6.15 pm 'mixed' from Woodstock. On Saturdays there was an additional late train between Oxford and Woodstock, which left Kidlington at 11.19 pm, reaching Woodstock by 11.27 pm; the final up departure left the terminus at 11.33 p.m. (This Saturday Only service was also worked by a steam railmotor.)

Freight Traffic and Freight Vehicles

Passenger bookings were relatively healthy during the Edwardian period, averaging around 17,000 tickets a year throughout the early 1900s. Goods traffic was, in general, of less importance and in 1903 Woodstock handled only 8,504 tons of freight, including 4,142 tons of coal, 2,421 tons of general merchandise and 1,740 tons of minerals. These figures remained more or less constant during the early 1900s, and by 1913 the station was still handling 17,168 passengers and 8,929 tons of freight a year.

Coal, the principal incoming freight, was distributed by local dealers such as Marriotts of Witney. Descended from Huguenot refugees who had fled from France to escape Catholic persecution, Marriotts had a surprisingly diverse range of business interests including blanketmaking, farming and dyeing, and coal distribution was just one branch of their overall activities. It was nevertheless quite extensive, and by the turn-of-the-century Marriotts owned two narrow boats, several road vehicles and at least eighteen coal wagons. These vehicles were used to convey coal from Midlands collieries to the firm's coal wharves at Woodstock, Witney, Eynsham, or other local stations, and they became a familiar feature on the branch. The wagons were repaired by Thomas Hunter of

BLENHEIM AND WOODSTOCK BRANCH

(WORKED BY ELECTRIC STAFF.)

Single Line between Blenheim and Woodstock and Kidlington.

DOWN TRAINS—WEEK DAYS.

Distance. M.	C.	STATIONS.		1	2	3	4	5	6	7	8	9
					B Mixed	B Pass.	B Mixed		B Pass.	B Pass.		B Pass.
					A.M.	A.M.	P.M.		P.M.	P.M.		P.M.
		Kidlington	dep.	..	8 20	10 48	12 53		3 48	6 47	..	9 30
3	57	Blenheim and Woodstock	arr.	....	8 30	10 56	1 3		3 56	6 55	....	9 38

UP TRAINS—WEEK DAYS.

STATIONS.		1	2	3	4	5	6	7	8	9
		B Pass.		B Pass.	B Pass.		B Mixed	B Mixed		B Pass.
		A.M.		A.M.	P.M.		P.M.	P.M.		P.M.
Blenheim and Woodstock	dep.	7 55	..	9 25	11 24	..	3 20	6 15		8 3[illegible]
Kidlington	arr.	8 3	....	9 33	11 32	....	3 30	6 26		8 38

Maximum Loads: Coal 12; Goods 18; Mixed 21.

BLENHEIM AND WOODSTOCK BRANCH

(WORKED BY ELECTRIC STAFF.)

Single Line between Blenheim and Woodstock and Kidlington.

DOWN TRAINS—WEEK DAYS.

Distance. M.	C.	STATIONS.		1	2	3	4	5	6	7	8	9	10
				B Mixed	B Pass.	B Mixed	B Excn. Q	B Motor Pass.	B Pass.	B Pass.	B Pass.	B Pass.	B Motor Pass. SO
				A.M.	A.M.	P.M.	P.M.	P.M.	P.M.	P.M.	P.M.	P.M.	P.M.
		Kidlington	dep.	8 20	11 0	12 53	*1 35*	2 9	3 48	5 51	6 47	9 31	*11 1[illegible]*
3	56	Blenheim and Woodstock	arr.	8 30	11 8	1 3	*1 43*	2 17	3 56	6 0	6 55	9 39	*11 [illegible]7*

UP TRAINS—WEEK DAYS.

STATIONS.		1	2	3	4	5	6	7	8	9	10
		B Pass.	B Pass.	B Pass.	B E'pty. Q	B Oxf'rd Motor Pass.	B Mixed	B Pass.	B Mixed	B Pass.	B Motor Pass. SO
		A.M.	A.M.	A.M.	P.M.	P.M.	P.M.	P.M.	P.M.	P.M.	P.M.
Blenheim and Woodstock ..	dep.	7 53	9 25	11 24	*1 20*	2 52	3 20	5 32	6 15	8 30	*11 [illegible]*
Kidlington	arr.	8 1	9 33	11 32	*1 28*	3 0	3 30	5 40	6 26	8 38	*11 [illegible]*

Maximum Loads: Coal 12; Goods 18; Mixed 21.

Q Tuesdays only, except on July 14th and 28th and September 22nd and 29th.

The May 1907 (top) and July 1908 working timetables.

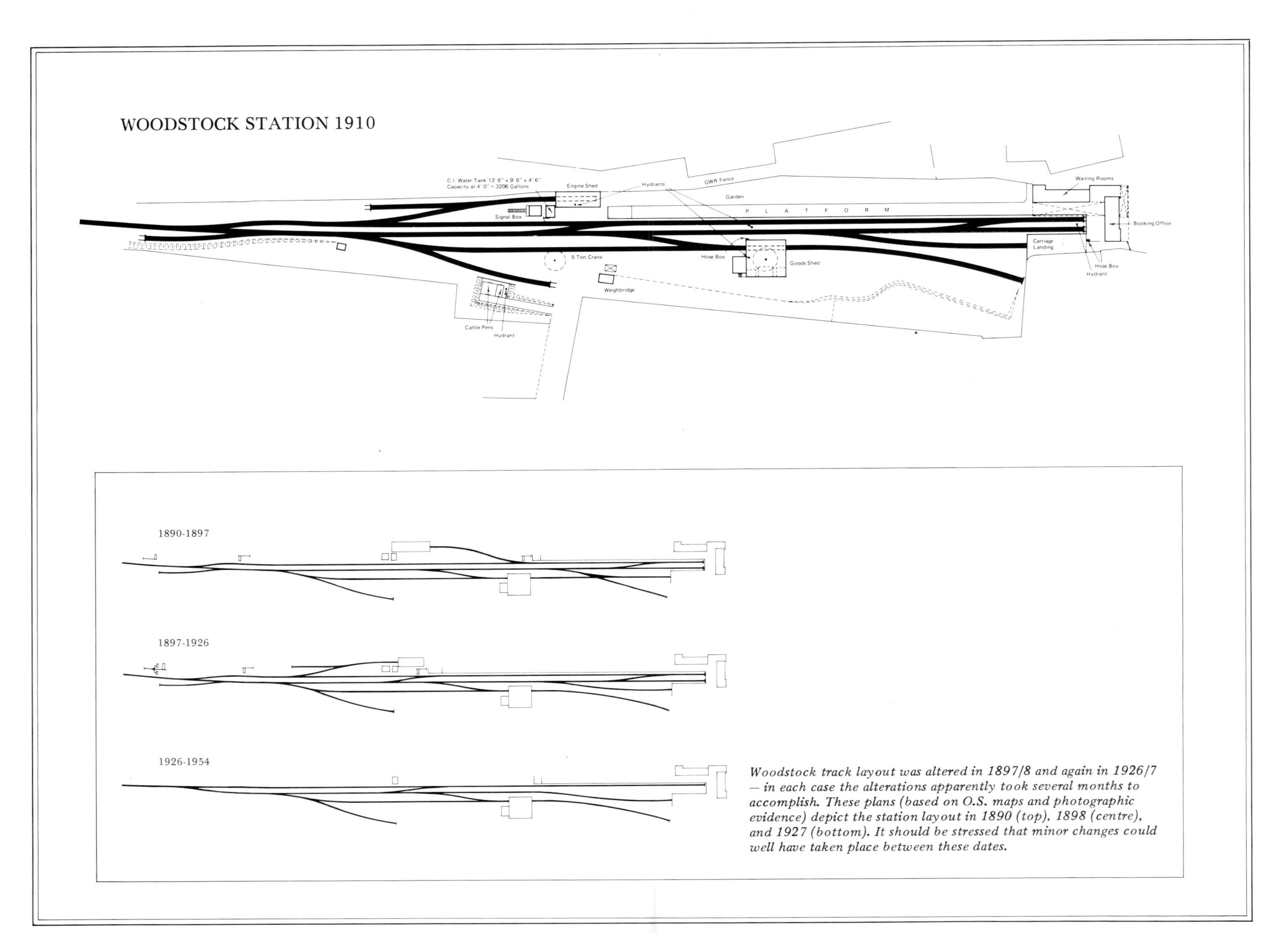

Woodstock track layout was altered in 1897/8 and again in 1926/7 – in each case the alterations apparently took several months to accomplish. These plans (based on O.S. maps and photographic evidence) depict the station layout in 1890 (top), 1898 (centre), and 1927 (bottom). It should be stressed that minor changes could well have taken place between these dates.

The station gardens, photographed from the loading dock in 1910. *British Railways*

Details of the beautiful garden arrangements, the right-hand view featuring one of the numerous standard GWR platform seats, here lettered 'BLENHEIM & WOODSTOCK' in shaded lettering. *British Railways*

'517' class 0–4–2T No. 1484 at Woodstock in the 1920s; guard Tommy Hine (with uniform hat) can be seen beside the clerestory roofed carriage. *Mrs. R. Giraud*

Rugby (who had probably also built them) and painted black with white lettering; in early days it is believed that the letters were shaded red.

On 15th April 1913 Marriotts wagon No 30 was derailed near Wolvercot, and it is interesting to find that the cost of rerailing it was £3 10s 6d — on top of which the GWR charged an additional £12 15s 8d for damage inflicted on the track. The offending vehicle was immediately sent to Rugby for repairs, and Hunters informed Marriotts that neither they, nor the owners, had been responsible for the accident; the vehicle had sustained considerable damage including bent axles, a broken journal and a smashed axle box — though the woodwork had 'not suffered so much'.

Coal was unloaded from the 'main' siding rather than from a short spur at the rear of the yard, and this sometimes caused friction when Bill Pomeroy, the regular Woodstock driver, violently shunted partially-full wagons, shaking coal from the open side doors and scattering it around the goods yard! On these occasions (which happened too frequently to have been mere accidents) Jack Wharton, the shunter-guard would thrown down his pole in frustration and temper.

Apart from coal, the line carried modest amounts of bricks, stone, timber, and general freight, together with consignments of raw skins for the local gloving trade. Outwards traffic included hampers of completed gloves and various agricultural products. Goods rolling stock seen at Woodstock reflected the limited range of traffic carried, and, generally speaking, coal and other 'opens' predominated. These were usually 7-plank coal wagons or 5-plank general merchandise vehicles — many of the latter were sheeted over with tarpaulins (and presumably carried sheep skins). In 1913 Marriotts considered fitting some of their own wagons with coke rails to give an increased capacity of 560 cubic ft, but it is not clear if this was actually carried out. Photographs show that Woodstock goods yard invariably contained a handful of 'Minks' or covered vans; these would have carried small consignments of general merchandise. Cattle were frequently moved in or out of Woodstock by train, and the station handled up to two hundred wagonloads of livestock a year.

Early Rationalisation

The heyday of the Woodstock branch spanned a period of just twenty-four years; a product of the settled, pre-World War One era, the line lost its *raison d'être* when that halcyon period ended abruptly on 4th August 1914. On that fateful day, the German army marched into neutral Belgium, and in response to a brutal, unprovoked attack on an inoffensive country, the British government declared war on the aggressors. Britain was not itself in danger, but the men of Woodstock (and every other town in the British Isles) were soon flocking to the colours in great numbers. The railway played its part in the conflict by carrying off scores of volunteers (and later conscripts) to the Western Front, and long lists of names on Woodstock and Bladon war memorials show that 55 husbands, fathers and brothers did not return.

The post-war world was a world in which great houses such as Blenheim had lost much of their former power and influence, and this obvious fact had several repercussions on Woodstock, its railway, and the Churchill family.

Lord Randolph had used his ancestral home for political advantage, but his son Winston was obliged to hide his aristocratic background — he was, after all, a democratic politician living in an egalitarian society. There were no more big political rallies and Blenheim assumed a purely local importance in the post-war era. Flower shows, fêtes and cricket matches were still held, but the days in which train-loads of party delegates would arrive at Woodstock station were gone forever. Tourists still came, but they could now travel by charabanc or private motor car, and, although the Great Western did much to publicise castles, abbeys, cathedrals and other tourist attractions served by its system, it did little to publicise Blenheim. On top of all this, the development of rural bus services started to attract shoppers and other local travellers from rail to road.

On the other hand, the inter-war years were a time of increasing leisure travel and although the Great Western did little to *actively* promote Blenheim as a mass tourist destination, the line's traffic returns show that Woodstock was, by 1923, carrying more passengers than in 1913. In fact Blenheim &

Woodstock station managed to retain its share of the passenger market at a time when comparable local stations were showing a decline, and this generally healthy trend is underlined by the table below, which compares Woodstock with two neighbouring GWR stations.

COMPARATIVE TRAFFIC FIGURES FOR WOODSTOCK AND OTHER STATIONS

Station	*Year*	*Receipts*	*Tickets*	*Goods tonnage*
Blenheim & Woodstock	1903	£5,386	17,436	8.504
Blenheim & Woodstock	1913	£5,610	17,168	8,929
Blenheim & Woodstock	1923	£9,376	19,117	11,450
Tetbury	1903	£9,747	17,664	13,046
Tetbury	1913	£10,875	17,809	15,464
Tetbury	1923	£13,385	14,043	10,826
Fairford	1903	£6,197	7,672	10,301
Fairford	1913	£6,413	6,882	9,154
Fairford	1923	£9,759	6,049	9,335

Such figures indicate that, if Woodstock was not the most profitable GWR rural branch line terminus, it was not, by any means, under-utilised. However, most bookings were for short distance journeys which yielded little income, and perhaps for this reason the branch was included in a survey of less profitable lines which was carried out in 1925. In all, some 53 branches were examined in an attempt to see where economies might be made, and for Woodstock the following picture emerged for the year under review:–

Passengers	Parcels	Goods	Totals	1924 Totals	Increase
£2,246	£947	£5,293	£8,486	£8,215	+ £271

Goods traffic included 8,276 tons of coal and minerals, together with 3,602 tons of general goods traffic; the station also handled 96 wagonloads of cattle and 2,336 cans of milk throughout 1925. Running costs were said to be £5,748 a year, representing 67.72% of the gross traffic receipts; the locomotive department absorbed £2,679 annually, while engineering expenses, signalling, lighting, water and rates

Station master Thomas Ashford beside his prize-winning station gardens in 1910. Mr. Ashford served at Blenheim & Woodstock for a quarter of a century. *British Railways*

BLENHEIM AND WOODSTOCK BRANCH

(WORKED BY ELECTRIC STAFF.)

Single Line between Blenheim and Woodstock and Kidlington.

DOWN TRAINS—WEEK DAYS.

Distance M.	Distance C.	STATIONS.	Sta'n No.	1 B	2 B	3 K	4 B	5 B	6 B	7 B	8 B	9 B	10 B	11 B
				Mixed	Pass.	Goods	Mixed	Oxf'rd Pass.	Pass.	Pass.	Pass.	Pass.	Pass.	Pass.
				A.M.	A.M.	A.M.	P.M.	P.M.	P.M.	P.M.	P.M.	P.M.	P.M.	P.M.
		Kidlington dep.	126	8 22	9 53	10 40	12 8	2 31	3 57	4 57	5 45	6 44	8 37	9 24
3	56	Blenheim & Woodstock arr.	180	8 32	10 0	10 50	12 18	2 41	4 5	5 5	5 53	6 52	8 45	9 32

UP TRAINS—WEEK DAYS.

Distance M.	Distance C.	STATIONS	Sta'n No.	1 B	2 B	3 K	4 B	5 B	6 B	7 B	8 K	9 B	10 B	11 B
				Pass.	Pass.	E & V	Mixed Pass.	Oxf'rd Pass.	Mixed	Pass.	Goods and C'ch's	Mixed	Pass.	Pass.
				A.M.	A.M.	A.M.	A.M.	P.M	P.M.	P.M.	P.M.	P.M.	P.M.	P.M.
		Blenheim and Woodstock dep.	126	7 52	9 23	10 13	11 22	1 7	3 25	4 35	5 20	6 15	8 17	9 0
3	56	Kidlington arr.	180	8 0	9 31	10 20	11 32	1 15	3 37	4 43	5 30	6 25	8 25	9 8

The 1923 working timetable.

amounted to £4,653 each year. Staffing absorbed another £1,095, which was estimated as 12.9% of the total expenditure for 1925. The report concluded that various small savings could be made if the following alterations were put into effect:–

1. The branch engine be transferred to Oxford and Woodstock shed be closed.
2. The track layout at Blenheim & Woodstock be reduced.
3. All services be worked by auto-trains.
4. Trains be worked without guards and Woodstock staff reduced.

It was estimated that these measures would save £324 a year. Accepting these conclusions in full, the Great Western withdrew conventional locomotive-hauled passenger trains in 1926 and introduced a revised timetable operated entirely by push-pull auto-trains. This enabled the track layout at Woodstock to be rationalised in various ways, the necessary trackwork being carried out in the summer of 1926. The new train service was based on Oxford rather than Woodstock and, with no need for a locomotive and train set to be stabled overnight, the branch engine shed was closed and subsequently demolished. Auto-trains did not require run-round facilities and the passenger loop at Woodstock was therefore lifted, leaving a residual, shorter loop for the daily goods service. What had hitherto been the engine release road then found a new use as a stabling siding, used mainly for goods vehicles (but occasionally for excursion stock). In all, this 1926 rationalisation involved the elimination of six turnouts, and left the western end of the terminus looking slightly 'empty' with an unnaturally-wide gap between two of its three remaining lines of rails.

Associated with this track rationalisation was the abolition of Blenheim & Woodstock signal box and all home and starter signals; henceforth the branch was worked by train staff on the 'one-engine-in-steam' principle, with only one train on the line at any given time. A single fixed distant was retained on the approach to Woodstock — and of course the approaches to Kidlington remained fully signalled. With the abolition of Woodstock signal box, the reduced track layout was controlled by two small ground frames strategically

A late 1920s or early 1930s view of Blenheim & Woodstock, looking west towards the buffers and showing the unusually wide spacing resulting from the 1926 track rationalisation. *L & GRP, cty. David & Charles*

A 1929 aerial shot of Woodstock station and goods yard. The sidings are, in this view, unusually full, and on close examination even the cattle dock is occupied by empty open wagons. This photograph is of particular interest in that it shows the goods yard entrance (extreme left). *Aerofilms*

positioned at either end of the remaining loop and designated Blenheim East and Blenheim West.

Train Services in the 1930s

The 'push-pull' train service called for few radical changes, and the branch still enjoyed a relatively good train service of nine trains each way daily, including two through services to Oxford. In general, this post-1926 service persisted, with only minor alterations until World War Two.

In 1937 the daily train service commenced with the arrival of a morning through train from Oxford which reached Kidlington at 7.23 am and arrived in Woodstock eight minutes later. The same locomotive and auto-trailer then made two return trips to Kidlington, with departures from Woodstock at 7.55 am and 9.15 am. At 10.30 am the engine was detached from its auto-trailer and proceeded to Kidlington with a single 'Toad' brake van which was restricted to the Woodstock line; having shunted Kidlington yard and picked-up any incoming goods vehicles, the branch freight returned at 11.10 am, arriving in Woodstock ten minutes later. There followed a further Woodstock–Kidlington round trip at 11.42 am, and, after performing any necessary shunting duties at Woodstock, the branch train then set off on an Oxford trip at 1.05 pm. Arriving back in Woodstock by 2.43 pm, the engine made two further return workings to Oxford and Kidlington at 3.25 pm and 4.33 pm respectively. The locomotive brought the Woodstock 'Toad' back at 5.50 pm prior to working two more round trips to the junction. Finally, at 9.55 pm the train returned to Oxford for servicing.

BLENHEIM AND WOODSTOCK BRANCH

AUTO CAR—ONE CLASS ONLY.

No Block Telegraph on this Line.
Form of Staff, round: Colour Red.

Single Line between Blenheim and Woodstock and Kidlington, worked by Train Staff and only one engine in steam at a time, or two coupled together.

DOWN TRAINS—WEEK DAYS ONLY.

Distance M.	Distance C.	STATIONS.	Ruling Gradient 1 in	B Oxf'd Auto.	B Mix'd	B Auto Pass.	K Goods	B Auto Pass.	B Oxf'rd Auto.	B Oxf'rd Auto	B Auto Pass.	G Eng'e & Van	B Auto Pass.	B Auto Pass.	
				A.M.	A.M	A.M.	A.M.	P.M.	P.M.	P.M.	P.M.	P.M.	P.M.	P.M	
		Kidlington dep	—	7 23	8 30	9 52	11 10	12 38 ‡	2 35	4 10	4 52	5 50	6 42	9 37	
2	9	Shipton-on-Cherwell Halt dep.	69 R	7 28	8 36	9 57	—	12 43 ‡	2 40	4 15	4 57	—	6 47	9 42	...
3	57	Blenheim & Woodstock arr.	129 R	7 31	8 40	10 0	11 20	12 46	2 43	4 18	5 0	RR 5 58	6 50	9 45	...

UP TRAINS—WEEK DAYS ONLY.

STATIONS.	Ruling Gradient 1 in	B Auto.	B Auto Pass.	G Eng'e & Van	B Auto Pass.	B Oxf'd Auto.	B Oxf'd Auto	B Auto Mixed	K Goods RR	B Auto Pass.	B Auto Pass.	B Oxf'd Auto.		
		A.M.	A.M.	A.M.	A.M.	P.M.	P.M.	P.M.	P.M.	P.M.	P.M.	P.M.		
Blenheim and Woodstock dep.	—	7 55	9 15	10 30	11 42	1 5	3 25	4 33	5 20	6 12 ‡	8 32	9 55	...	...
Shipton-on-Cherwell Halt dep.	129 F	7 58	9 18	—	11 45	1 8	3 28	4 37	—	6 15	8 35	9 58	...	...
Kidlington arr.	69 F	8 3	9 23	10 38	11 50	1 13	3 33	4 43	5 30	62 0	8 40	10 3	...	...

‡ May run as a Mixed trip when necessary at point to point times shewn for other Mixed trips. When 12.38 p.m. Kidlington run as "Mixed" the 10.30 a.m. Blenheim and 11.10 a.m. Kidlington will not run.

Taken from 1937 Working Timetable

It will be seen that, even after rationalisation, the Woodstock branch service remained relatively complex, yet this service of nine passenger trains, one goods trip and one light engine working, was accomplished by the use of just one locomotive, one auto-trailer and one brake van on what was, in effect, an unsignalled 'basic' railway. From the ordinary traveller's point of view the resulting service provided useful local transport facilities, the limited number of through trips to Oxford being especially valued. The early afternoon through service was particularly popular with shoppers, and, as the return fare was only 6d, this working was always known as the 'Woolworth Special' or 'Woolworth Express' (in those days, as older readers will know, nothing in Woolworth's cost over 6d).

Unfortunately, rival motor bus services posed a small, but growing threat to the branch throughout the 1930s — the buses *all* ran through to Oxford, offering a greater choice of destinations within the city boundary; rail travellers, in contrast, were faced with an annoying change at Kidlington, followed by a long and boring walk from Oxford station to the city centre. Some potential travellers may have found the railway more convenient — particularly local glove workers, who, in the 1930s, found employment in a new glove factory in Riverside Road, not far from Oxford station; sadly the Great Western did little to encourage these daily travellers to use the trains, and no morning through service was provided. Similarly, returning workers were not offered an evening Oxford-Woodstock service, and in retrospect one wonders why the GWR could not have arranged a more useful range of Oxford services. In spite of these apparent deficiencies, branch passenger traffic remained buoyant. It is true that Woodstock issued only 13,003 tickets throughout 1931, but thereafter the annual figures rose progressively, reaching 15,023 in 1932 and 23,295 in 1933; goods traffic, on the other hand, was far more vulnerable to road competition, and by 1933 the station was handling only 2,784 tons of freight a year.

New Sources of Traffic in the later GW Period

Although the 1930s were a time of acute depression, there were one or two brave attempts to bring employment and increased prosperity to Oxfordshire, and in 1923 a bacon factory was built on a site near Kidlington station that had formerly been occupied by a timber yard. Originally used by Oxford Farmers Ltd, the site was rail-connected — a new siding being laid across the station approach road. The GWR agreed that the cost of this siding — estimated at about £850 — would be refunded to Oxford Farmers by means of a 5% rebate on all traffic for a period not exceeding ten years, but unfortunately the factory was not a success and the 1932 *Little Guide to Oxfordshire* noted that the venture had failed. By 1934, however, the business had been revived by C & T Harris Ltd of Calne, and Kidlington was once again receiving cattle for slaughter and despatching consignments of bacon from its private siding.

Another new, and at first promising source of freight traffic was sugar beet — much of which was sent from Woodstock to a new factory at Eynsham, on the Witney branch. Opened in 1928, this new venture did much to stimulate interest in beet as a cash crop, but sadly the Eynsham factory was unsuccessful, and was closed in 1931.

In retrospect these additional sources of agricultural traffic did little to help the branch — there was, on the other hand, a potential source of *bulk* traffic which might have given the

Fair Rosamund and auto-car No. 119 after arrival at Blenheim & Woodstock in May 1930; the engine had, by that time, acquired a full cab. *H. C. Casserley*

An unidentified '517' class 0–4–2T (probably No. 1159) propelling its single auto-car out of Blenheim & Woodstock station on 8th August 1935. *R. W. Kidner, courtesy Oakwood Press*

Woodstock line a new lease of life. Quarrying had long been carried out in the area, and there were stone quarries at Stonesfield (to the west of Woodstock) and at Kirtlington (to the north-east). Later, a small limestone quarry was opened at Shipton-on-Cherwell by Messrs Lamprey of Banbury. In 1906 the Oxford Portland Cement Company opened a quarry and cement works on a site at Kirtlington, some two miles north of the branch; initially cement was despatched entirely by canal — though in later years some consignments were transferred to rail via private sidings at Bletchington (i.e. the original 'Woodstock Road' station).

Demand for building materials in the 1920s led to formation of the Oxford & Shipton Cement Company and the opening of a much larger quarry and works on a new site, immediately to the north of Shipton-on-Cherwell village. The chosen site was a 'V' shaped wedge of land between the Woodstock and Banbury lines, leading to speculation that quarry sidings might be entered via the branch. In this context it is interesting to note that the eastern extremity of the Woodstock Railway had been built to accommodate a double track, and for this reason the canal bridge at Shipton-on-Cherwell was given twin abutments; it would therefore have been a simple matter to arrange access to the works by laying a loop from the branch to the main line at Bletchington. In the event, access was arranged by provision of a series of loops alongside the main line, some 1 mile 42 chains north of Kidlington, and, although the branch ran alongside the quarry, no physical link was ever established.

The main line exchange sidings were installed in November 1927, and these were initially used during construction of the plant. Two kilns were supplied by Edgar Allen Ltd, each being 200 ft long and 9 ft in diameter, and a futuristic new factory was soon taking shape in the peaceful Cherwell Valley. Production began in 1929, and the Shipton Cement Works inevitably became an important employer of labour in an otherwise rural area.

A whole community of cement workers was created at 'Bunkers Hill', where the company erected several rows of well-built 1920s-style houses on a rather isolated site, and, to serve the needs of this settlement, the GWR opened a halt between Woodstock and Kidlington on 1st April 1929. Known as Shipton-on-Cherwell Halt (though it was some distance from Shipton village) this new stopping-place was perched somewhat precariously atop an embankment, immediately west of the Oxford—Banbury road bridge; access from ground level was by means of a sloping cinder path. The new

The newly built cement workers' dwellings at Bunkers Hill were within easy walking distance of Shipton-on Cherwell Halt. The well wooded appearance of this part of Oxfordshire has since been lost with the ravages of Dutch Elm Disease.

Packer Collection, Oxfordshire Museum Services, Woodstock

The branch auto-train enters Shipton-on-Cherwell Halt. *J. H. Russell*

The wrought iron girder bridge which carried the branch across the Banbury Road at Shipton-on-Cherwell. The 'kissing-gate' gave access to the halt. *W. A. Camwell*

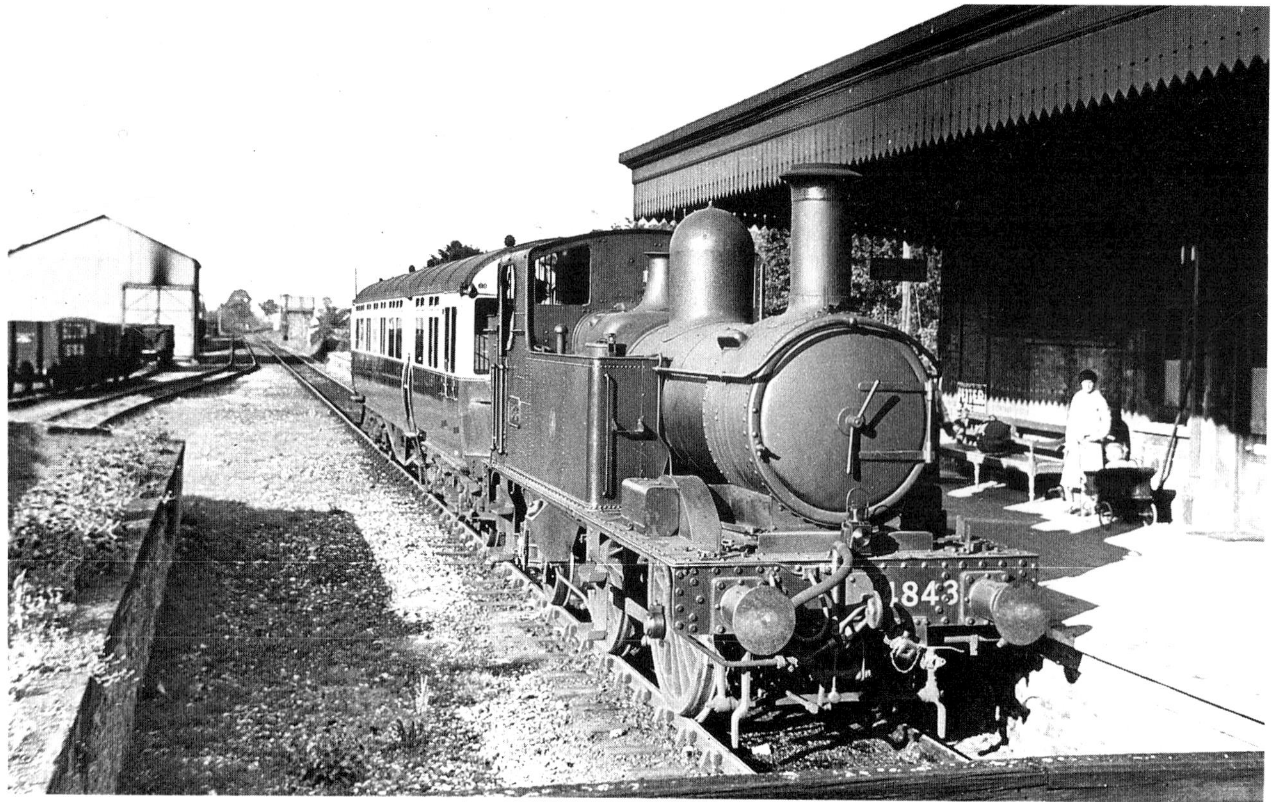

'48XX' (later '14XX') class 0–4–2T No. 4843 entering Blenheim & Woodstock station on 24th June 1935. *F. M. Butterfield*

halt was soon carrying significant numbers of travellers from Bunkers Hill and Shipton old village, and with no competing bus routes Shipton-on-Cherwell Halt was soon boosting branch ticket sales. (Shipton's traffic receipts were not published separately, but it seems likely that a rise in Woodstock's passenger figures from 17,000 in the early 1900s to 22,000+ in the 1930s was attributable, at least in part, to the new halt.)

In 1935 the withdrawal of *Fair Rosamund* marked an important break with the past — for, as we have seen, this engine had worked on the line since the 1890s and was therefore a tangible link with the original Woodstock Railway. Other '517' Class engines, including Nos 1159 and 1484, had worked on the branch from time to time, but for many older people 'Rosie' had become almost a living entity. There were, not surprisingly, suggestions that her nameplates could be transferred to a new engine, but the Great Western authorities did not really approve of such unofficial local namings, and the name *Fair Rosamund* did not reappear until the 1970s (when it was revived and given to Oxford-based Class 47 No 47510).

Fair Rosamund was replaced by new but substantially similar engines of the Collett '48XX' 0–4–2T Class. Introduced in 1932, the '48XX' (later '14XX') Class was a modernised version of the '517' Class, with 5 ft 2 in coupled wheels and 16 in × 24 in cylinders. Designed specifically for auto-working, the '48XXs' became standard motive power on the Woodstock line for the last few years of its existence; regular engines in the pre-war years included Nos 4850 and

Fair Rosamund waiting at Oxford station on 21st June 1930. *F. J. Agar*

4843, together with '517' Class 0–4–2T No 1159 (which survived her sister *Fair Rosamund* by several years).

If the Woodstock branch had its 'regular' locomotives, the same cannot be said with regard to auto-trailers; the Great Western built several varieties of auto-coach, and most types seem to have appeared on the branch at one time or another. In the 1920s, car No 99 was often used, and this vehicle was of particular interest in that it was a railmotor conversion (that is to say a former steam railmotor from which the powered bogie had been removed). Built in the early 1900s, No 99 was one of the early railmotors with vertical sides. Photographs show that similar vehicles Nos 110 and 119 were frequently used during the 1930s; all three trailers were 57 ft cars containing two open saloons, one for smokers, the other for non-smokers. The auto-cars were 'one class only' vehicles, with no first class accommodation, and all the cars featured retractable steps on either side — a relic of the original Great Western 'haltes' which had no raised platforms. It is said that on occasions (and strictly unofficially) trains would be stopped at recognised points *en route* to Woodstock, thereby giving regular travellers a true 'door to door' service! Unfortunately this practice resulted in the loss of several sets of steps when hapless guards forgot to retract them after such unofficial request stops.

In the 1930s the Great Western built some modern steel-panelled auto-coaches which, like their predecessors, were 57 ft one-class vehicles containing two open saloons. At least one of the 1930s batch — No 187 — appeared on the Woodstock line, but such modernity was not destined to last and before very long further railmotor conversions had appeared, including some high-capacity 70 ft vehicles that had initially been designed for use on London Division suburban lines.

Freight vehicles seen at Woodstock during the 'thirties were predominantly vans and 'opens', with Marriotts' PO wagons still much in evidence. Other private owner wagons included a small fleet of two vehicles owned by Scarsbrooks of Woodstock. In theory, these should perhaps have been numbered 1 and 2, but Mr Scarsbrook decided to give them the numbers 15 and 20 because these happened to be the ages of his two sons when the wagons were first delivered. Painted dark red, they had white lettering, and were maintained by specialist wagon repairers for an annual fee of £5 a year.

Fair Rosamund rounding the curve at Shipton-on-Cherwell with a mixed working in the 1930s. *J. E. Kite*

Rural Delivery Services and The Area Served by Woodstock Station

When first opened, the Woodstock branch had been in competition with an extensive network of local carrier routes, but after a short time a *modus vivendi* became established in which the carriers called *en route* at Woodstock station to pick up parcels or small consignments of goods for delivery to outlying villages. In the early 1900s, for example, William Knibbs and William Willoughby both provided surprisingly complex carrier services based on Woodstock; on Thursdays they travelled to Witney, on other days Oxford, and it was no trouble for them to travel a short distance from their normal routes in order to serve isolated farms or cottages.

Traditionally, these carrier services were maintained by carts or wagons — often fitted with canvas covers to protect goods or passengers from the elements. Regular timetables were adhered to, and the carriers called at regular 'stations' or stops (usually local inns). In addition to these 'informal' road feeder services, the GWR also entered into contracts with specific carriers in order that Blenheim & Woodstock residents would be guaranteed a door-to-door delivery service, and on 1st December 1908 Mary Jane Guy agreed to provide cartage facilities up to a distance of one mile from Woodstock. Later, on 1st March 1922, Frederick Dodwell (of Market Street, Woodstock) entered into a similar cartage agreement, which remained in force for several years and was not officially terminated until 1949.

In later years some more enterprising carriers retired their horses and changed to motor vehicles — among them Mr Knibbs whose converted 'Model T' delivery lorry is still remembered by older residents of Combe, Woodstock and Handborough.

The Great Western invested heavily in motorised delivery vehicles during the 1920s and 1930s, and, by analogy with other GW termini, Woodstock should have become a centre for local road transport operations. Unfortunately, the Woodstock line was surrounded by main line stations such as Heyford, Handborough and Kidlington, and these neighbouring stations had their own road delivery vehicles which tended to 'compete' with Blenheim & Woodstock.

This competition is underlined by a 1938 Great Western staff publication known as the book of *Towns Villages & Outlying Works*, which showed 'at a glance' the station to which parcels should be consigned and the delivery arrangements available at each destination. Bladon, for example, was one mile from Handborough by carrier, two miles from Blenheim &

A general view of Blenheim & Woodstock station in the 1930s, showing a mixture of GWR and LMS goods stock on the shed road.
Author's Collection

Woodstock by carrier, five miles from Eynsham by railway delivery lorry and six miles from Oxford by bus. Faced with this information, most consigning stations would have sent parcels to that particular location via Handborough rather than Woodstock, thereby depriving Woodstock of traffic. Similarly, villages to the north-east of Woodstock (such as Kirtlington) were served by GWR lorry services from Bletchington. The unfortunate inhabitants of Shipton-on-Cherwell, Thrupp and Bunker's Hill had no delivery services of any description, but Kidlington residents were served by a cartage service from their own station (though, as the village and its station were a mile apart, the service was not free). The people of Woodstock, in contrast, enjoyed a free cartage service from Blenheim & Woodstock station, and the Woodstock lorry also provided a free service to Old Woodstock and Hensington (both, in effect, outlying parts of Woodstock). Blenheim Palace was within the 'free cartage' area, but the scattered cottages in Blenheim Park had to pay for deliveries. Northwards, isolated villages such as Wootton, Glympton and Kiddington were still served by private carriers from Woodstock.

The fact that the Great Western did *not* provide its own country lorry service suggests that traffic emanating from these villages was negligible, and this in turn suggests that Woodstock's sundries and parcels business was neither extensive nor lucrative. Although Blenheim & Woodstock station was to some extent a freight and parcels distribution centre for the surrounding area its 'hinterland' was unusually small, and did not extend far beyond the limited boundaries of Woodstock and the adjoining parish of Hensington; in an age of growing 'bus and lorry competition this did not bode well for the future. (The area served from Woodstock station is shown in the table below.)

GOODS and PARCELS DELIVERY ARRANGEMENTS IN THE WOODSTOCK AREA 1938–1954

Name of Place	*Distance from Woodstock*	*Delivery arrangements*
Bladon*	2 miles	private carrier
Blenheim Palace	¾ mile	free cartage service
Blenheim Park	3 miles	cartage service/carriers
Glympton	4 miles	private carrier
Hensington Within	¼ mile	free cartage service
Hensington Without	1 mile	free cartage service
Kiddington*	4 miles	private carrier
Woodstock	—	free cartage service
Wootton*	3 miles	private carrier

*= Also served by railway lorries from Handborough, Bletchington or Oxford

Perhaps surprisingly, the area served by Marriotts, Scarsbrooks and other local coal merchants was relatively large, and research carried out by J.R. Bond of the City & County Museum, Woodstock, indicates that (in addition to the outlying villages of Glympton and Wootton) the neighbouring villages of Tackley, Shipton-on-Cherwell, Begbroke, Combe and Yarnton were also served by Woodstock-based coal merchants, whilst Bladon, Stonesfield and Kidlington were served partly by Woodstock and partly by nearby main line stations. This anomalous situation had arisen because local coal dealers found Woodstock more convenient than

Handborough — moreover, the fact that Blenheim & Woodstock had a well laid-out goods yard providing sufficient room for the merchants' coal wharves and offices made it a more attractive operating base than either Kidlington or Bletchington stations (both of which had very cramped goods yards).

By collating Woodstock's rural delivery area with its coal service area, a clearly-defined 'hinterland' emerges; significantly this was a roughly triangular segment of land between the OW & WR and Oxford & Rugby lines. None of the villages served were more than four miles from Woodstock station, and most of these small settlements were also served by other passenger or goods stations (see accompanying map).

Horse-drawn delivery vehicles were probably still in use in the mid-1930s, but in 1938 a new 20-ton weighbridge was installed in Blenheim & Woodstock goods yard because the existing 7 ton cart weighing machine could not handle heavier motor lorries. The new machine had an 18 ft plate, and its appearance suggests that motor vehicles were introduced at the end of 1937 or the beginning of 1938.

Tales of the Line

The Woodstock branch was an integral part of everyday life for over sixty years, and in that time it became the subject of jokes, legends and local folk-lore. For example, one or two drivers were gardening enthusiasts, and if they needed any bean-sticks they would occasionally back the train along the line after depositing passengers at Woodstock; the best sticks were found in the deep cutting between Woodstock and Shipton, and, having spotted some likely saplings, the drivers concerned would halt their train and start cutting sticks, which would later be taken back to Oxford stacked in the coal bunker. Rabbits, too, could be found in the cutting, and some drivers are alleged to have set traps in the hope of obtaining an extra ingredient for their cooking pot! Many tales involve Bill Pomeroy, who worked on the line for over thirty years and became well-known to regular travellers; when driving from the trailer he would sometimes leave his controls and retire to the passenger saloons where he could chat to his many friends and acquaintances.

Other stories relate to the 'school' trains which took senior children from Woodstock to Oxford High, Magdalen College or other secondary schools in Oxford. (With no grammar school in either Woodstock or Kidlington, parents wishing to give their children a decent education had to pay for them to attend public schools in Oxford as day scholars.) In 1932 the High School opted for council control but the numbers of Woodstock children attending Oxford schools remained small and highly select. Like other élite groups, this small band of youthful commuters evolved several initiation ceremonies — such as burying new pupils under seat cushions on their first journey to school! There was at one time segregation of boys and girls, but daredevils would imitate Robert Donat in *The Thirty Nine Steps* by climbing along the sides of their trains to reach the female coach — this was a relatively easy operation in the days when some old vehicles still had continuous running boards!

When travelling to Oxford in time to reach school it was necessary to change *en route* at Kidlington; similarly on the return journey children would catch a Banbury local to the junction, where their own train would be waiting in its bay. The two trains would often depart simultaneously, resulting in what appeared to be a neck and neck 'race' between 'Rosie' and the 'Banbury Stopper'. On such occasions schoolboy travellers would cheer their own trains — knowing, however, that 'Rosie' would always lose when she slowed for Thrupp curve!

'Rosie' and Other Local Names

The trains themselves had several local nicknames, 'Rosie' being the most popular. Woodstock people usually pronounced it 'Roz-zie', not 'Rose-ey' — the name being short for Rosamund rather than Rosemary; occasionally, some Woodstock residents will still speak of the 'Woolworth Express' as if this was a generic term for the whole line and not just the mid-day through trip. The usual nickname for Oxfordshire branch trains was 'The Flyer', whereas in Berkshire auto-trains were often called 'bunks'; both may have been used to a limited extent on the Woodstock line — though it is possible that those who asked the time of 'The Woodstock Flyer' or 'The Woodstock Bunk' were not natives of the district and did not know that 'Rosie' was the *correct* name!

World War Two

On 3rd September 1939 the people of Woodstock heard on their 'wireless' sets that Herr Hitler had rejected Britain's ultimatum to cease hostilities in Poland, and that in consequence Britain was at war with Germany. Many listeners expected the skies to fill with Luftwaffe bombers within the first few days, but, in the event, the initial months of the war were strangely quiet. For railway travellers, a reduction in services and the sight of servicemen hurrying to join their ships and units were reminders that there was a 'war on'. A nightly blackout was put into effect, and to stop travellers from falling from the edges of darkened platforms a broad white line was hastily applied along each platform edge. In the slightly unreal conditions of 'The Phoney War', curious and often humorous rumours began to gain credence, and there was much talk of 'Fifth Columnists' who had supposedly been parachuted into Britain disguised as bird-watchers, monks, nuns, and other unlikely characters!

The Fall of France in June 1940 dispelled any illusions about the gravity of the situation, and, fearing imminent invasion, the government ordered that all road signs and station nameboards should be taken down. Obstructions were placed in fields and open spaces to impede airborne landings, and able-bodied males were encouraged to join the Local Defence Volunteers (renamed the Home Guard in July 1940). The war had, in effect, entered a 'Napoleonic' phase in which Britain stood alone against an armed and largely hostile Europe — and with several RAF stations in the vicinity Woodstock was inevitably drawn in to the aerial battle that commenced in August 1940.

The largest local aerodrome was situated just one mile south of the Woodstock branch. Known as RAF Kidlington (although it was actually nearer Woodstock), this airfield had opened as a civilian flying school in the 1930s, becoming an RAF station in December 1939. Like most Oxfordshire aerodromes, it was primarily a training establishment, initially equipped with Hawker Harts, Harvards and Airspeed Oxfords. A second airfield, confusingly known as RAF Woodstock, was opened at Starveal Farm, some 2 miles north-west of the town; this was used as a storage landing ground by 41 Group, Maintenance Command, and its aircraft were secretly dispersed over a wide area, concealed beneath camouflage netting and hidden in local woodlands. Other aerodromes were situated at Kiddington and Kirtlington, to the north-west and north-east of Woodstock respectively; RAF Kiddington was a Relief Landing Ground for Kidlington, while Kirtlington (sometimes called Middleton) was another storage ground for new or repaired aircraft.

With so many RAF stations in the area, it might be supposed that the Woodstock branch carried much extra traffic, but this was not necessarily the case, and published figures suggest that the branch carried *less* passenger traffic during the war than it had carried in the 1930s; in 1933, for example, Blenheim & Woodstock station had issued 23,295 tickets, but it issued only 19,500 in 1943, falling to 17,500 in 1945. In general, the railways carried 70% more passengers and 50% more freight in World War Two, but the above figures suggest that little extra traffic flowed along the Woodstock branch.

The Oxford to Birmingham main line, in contrast, was worked to its limits throughout the war, becoming a vital rail artery between London and the North. Extra refuge sidings and loops were added at several places, and Oxford became a major railway centre, with new marshalling yards at Hinksey, to the south of the city, and Yarnton to the north. The Oxford to Wolvercot section was frequently congested, and to ease this problem an extra down line was installed between Oxford station and Wolvercot Junction. At Kidlington, the presence of the Woodstock branch provided a ready-made down running loop, and a new crossover was added to link the branch and the down main line near Thrupp; these alterations were completed at a cost of £3,460, this sum being reimbursed by H.M. Government.

With so many military targets in the area, it was inevitable that Luftwaffe bombers would pay an occasional call and on 1st November 1940 a lone raider dropped four bombs on Kidlington aerodrome, destroying two Harvard trainers and damaging a hangar. On 14th November local inhabitants may have been awakened by the distinctive and sinister sound of German bombers as they crossed West Oxfordshire from south to north *en route* for Coventry; on these occasions incendiary devices were dropped over a wide area, presumably by enemy 'pathfinder' squadrons. Neither Oxford nor Woodstock were damaged, though on 13th August 1941 RAF Kidlington was bombed once again.

In 1942, Kidlington, Kiddington, and other local airfields commenced glider training in preparation for the eventual D-Day landings, and in the next few months curious observers might have spotted Hotspur gliders being towed around the skies above Woodstock by various unlikely 'tugs' (including Hector and Audax biplanes!). By 1944 the entire area had become a vast military camp, intimately connected with airborne forces; every road and lane was filled by military vehicles, parked nose-to-tail along the grass verges, and there were supply dumps all around Woodstock, including a large bomb storage area between Bladon and Handborough.

Meanwhile, Blenheim Palace was being put to a variety of emergency uses. At the start of the war it had accommodated evacuated schoolboys from Malvern College, but as the war effort got into its full stride the palace provided a home for MI5 and (more prosaically) The Ministry of Supply. With much of the vast interior occupied by desks, filing cabinets and other office equipment, some departments were moved into temporary huts in the forecourt; nearby, army vehicles were stored in the park, and on one memorable occasion tracked personnel carriers were seen to emerge from the lake! With private transport severely restricted, all railways carried extra traffic, and, with so many military and government personnel billeted in the town, Woodstock station was no doubt used by at least some servicemen and civil servants going on leave or returning to their duties. Another source of wartime traffic stemmed from the employment of skilled Woodstock glove workers in Oxford — many of whom travelled daily to and from their work (though some at least would have commuted by bus).

In retrospect, these additional forms of traffic were carried at a time when road transport was poised to do irreparable damage to the Woodstock branch and, although the line's *ordinary* traffic continued to decrease throughout the early 1940s, military traffic must have done much to keep Woodstock station in business. However, soldiers, sailors and airmen travelling on official duty used 'warrants' which were presented at the booking office in return for tickets, and it is likely that when charges were calculated, small stations such as Woodstock were not counted as 'issuing stations' for such tickets — the extra wartime traffic may not feature in Woodstock's receipts. In any case, when the war ended in 1945 the branch carried no further military traffic. So long as private transport was restricted, this posed no major problem, but as soon as life started to return to normal it was clear that the branch — barely profitable even in the 1930s — would have a struggle to survive in the post-war era.

Kidlington station was, it seems, used to a much greater extent than Blenheim & Woodstock, especially by airmen based at the neighbouring aerodrome whose hutted accommodation was merely a short stroll away down Langford Lane. There were also occasional consignments of heavy freight for the RAF, and it was perhaps for this reason that the Great Western was called upon to send mobile 6-ton cranes to the station during the critical 'D-Day' month of June 1944; it remains a matter of conjecture why these machines should have been needed, but in retrospect it is possible that as the invasion gathered momentum, extra Hotspur Gliders may have been urgently needed by the RAF, and some could have been transported by rail via Kidlington. In addition to the main airfield site to the north of Langford Lane, there was also a maintenance unit on the opposite side of the road, and, as the war effort got into its stride, the private siding used by C & T Harris Ltd was pressed into emergency use by the Air Ministry (presumably to ease congestion in the goods yard proper).

Wartime passenger and freight services were similar to those provided in the 1930s, and there was no radical cut in services, the only significant alteration being a reduction in the number of Oxford workings from three down and two up in 1941/42 to just two up and two down by 1943. On Saturdays, however, there was an increase to three up and three down through trips, and although the evening up service was officially an 'empty stock' working once it

'517' class 0–4–2T No. 1159 entering Blenheim & Woodstock station. *J. H. Russell*

reached Kidlington, it is rumoured that airmen occasionally begged the odd lift into Oxford.

The return of peace in 1945 was followed by a rundown of all local RAF stations, and this led, in turn, to a marked reduction in branch passenger traffic. The wartime timetable persisted, however, with only minor alterations, and the pattern of services provided in May 1946 was little different to that in force since 1926. In 1947 the line was affected by heavy snowfalls, and at the end of that year the Great Western period drew to a somewhat muted close.

Having chronicled the history of the line from its inception until the eve of nationalisation, it would now be appropriate to interrupt the main story in order to take an imaginary journey over the line as it would have appeared at the very end of its life. The next chapter will therefore describe such a journey.

'517' class 0–4–2T No. 1159 beside the wooden platform at Shipton-on-Cherwell. *J. H. Russell*

SKETCH MAP OF THE WOODSTOCK BRANCH

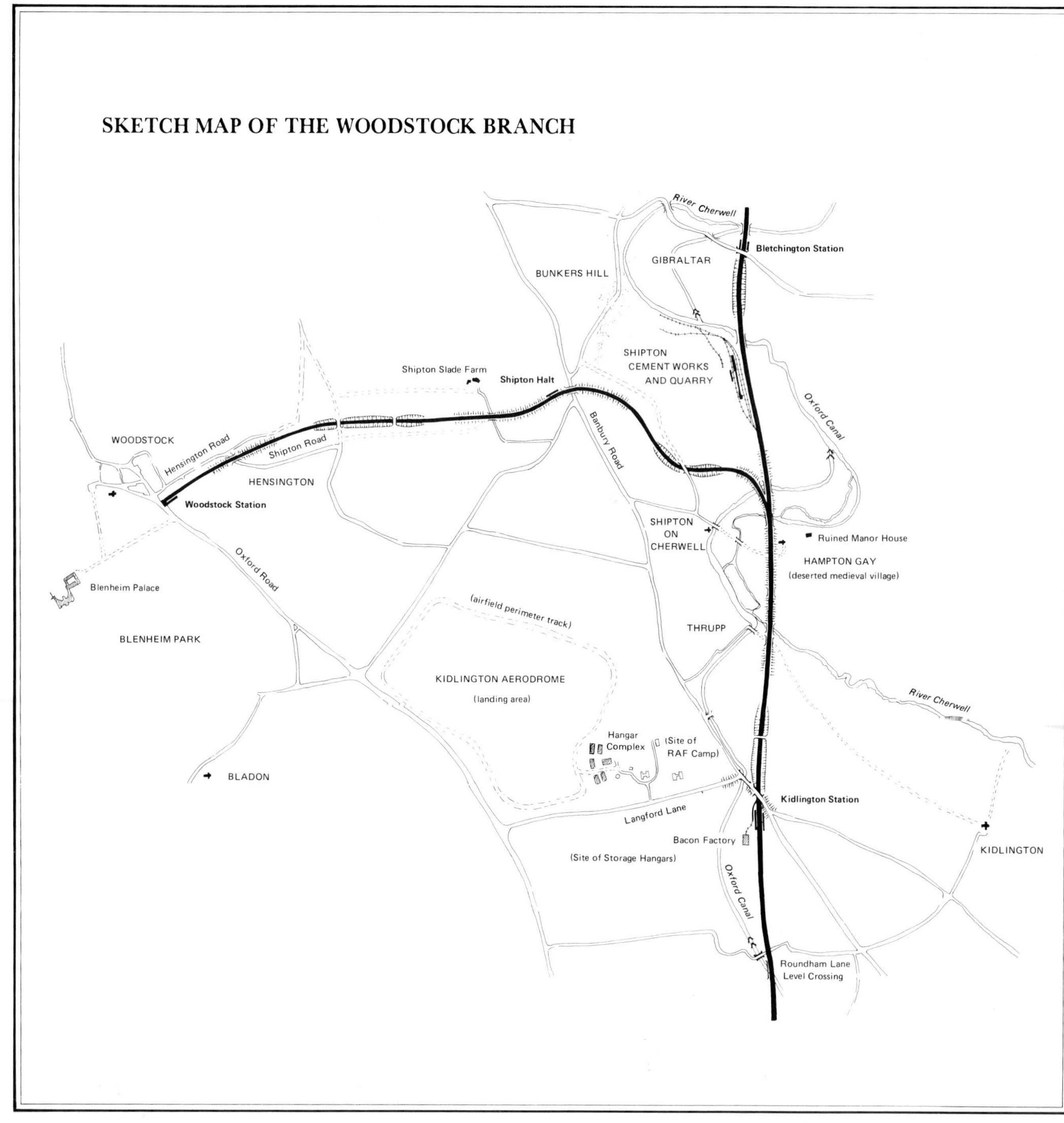

CHAPTER FIVE

THE ROUTE DESCRIBED

WHEN first planned, the Blenheim & Woodstock branch had been seen as the northern extremity of a 9½ mile route from Oxford, but, as mentioned earlier, the GWR chose to operate the branch as a self-contained route between Woodstock and Kidlington. There were nevertheless *some* through workings, and in 1926 Oxford became the stabling point for branch locomotives and passenger rolling stock; it is appropriate therefore to take this main line station as the start of an imaginary journey to Blenheim & Woodstock.

Woodstock services commenced their journeys from a bay at the northern end of Oxford's down platform. When opened on 12th June 1844 the Oxford branch had terminated in a small station in St Aldate's, and the station used by Woodstock trains was not opened until 1st October 1852, when the Oxford to Birmingham main line was opened throughout. This second station was of wooden construction with a Brunelian overall roof spanning its two platform roads and two central goods lines. In 1910 the layout was extended, and, having lost its barn-like wooden roof, Oxford gained lengthened up- and down-platforms and an additional bay on the up side. An unusual feature of this revised layout were the two scissors crossovers at the centre of the station, allowing two trains into each platform at the same time. To the east of the Great Western, and on a slightly lower level, was a rival London & North Western station, the terminus of a 31¼ mile branch from the West Coast main line at Bletchley.

Leaving Oxford station, Woodstock trains crossed a maze of pointwork, passing the wooden GWR engine sheds to the left and the brick-built L & NWR shed to the right. Locomotive enthusiasts would note an impressive range of motive power in and around these two sheds, including Great Western 'Saint', 'Hall' and 'Star' Class 4–6–0s, '28XX' 2–8–0s, '63XX' 2–6–0s, '61XX' 2–6–2Ts, '45XX' 2–6–2Ts, '56XX' 0–6–2Ts, '57XX' 0–6–0PTs, '54XX' 0–6–0PTs and '14XX' 0–4–2Ts. The L & NWR shed housed a contrasting assortment of ex-LNW and Midland classes such as 'Precursor' 2–4–0s, 'G2' 0–8–0s, 'Coal Tank' 0–6–2Ts, '2P' 4–4–0s, '3F' 0–6–0Ts and '4F' 0–6–0s; the North Western shed was a 'northlight' pattern structure, whereas the GW depot consisted of two pre-fabricated 'Brunel' style gabled sheds.

Gaining speed, the auto-trains ran north along the quadruple-tracked Great Western main line, with the double track L & NWR route running parallel to the east. Beyond, the terraced houses of 'Jericho' lined the level horizon; this working-class Victorian settlement provided homes for many

The Woodstock branch train waiting in Oxford's down bay platform; trains normally arrived in the up main and then crossed to the down bay prior to forming the next departure for Woodstock. *Dr. G. D. Parkes*

A rare view of Wolvercot Halt, showing a characteristic Great Western pagoda shed. *Lens of Sutton*

of Oxford's railwaymen, and was also the home of Hardy's fictional hero, Jude Fawley. The tall, cement-rendered tower of St Barnabus Church (which featured in *Jude the Obscure* as 'St Silas') was a notable landmark above the roof-tops. The trains soon passed Oxford North Junction Signal Box, which controlled entry to the GW engine sheds and goods loops; in 1942 a connecting link was installed here to provide through running facilities onto the ex-LNW line.

Continuing northwards, trains crossed the flat, low-lying expanse of Port Meadow, with the Oxford Canal to the east and the River Thames away to the west; in the distance the wooded shape of Wytham Hill added interest to an otherwise featureless scene. Nearing Wolvercot, the Bletchley line turned north-eastwards to cross the flat, marshy region known as Otmoor, while the Great Western curved gradually to the north-west.

With the willow-lined banks of the Thames now clearly visible to the left, trains reached the site of Wolvercot Platform, a closed halt situated some 2 miles 25 chains from Oxford. Up and down platforms were provided here, together with a single siding on the down side of the line which was used mainly for hay traffic from Port Meadow. The siding may also have been used to tranship loads to and from a nearby Oxford Canal wharf, and in this context it is significant that a relatively powerful 3-ton crane was provided.

Although only a 'halt', Wolvercot had once been staffed and in World War One it became the first local station to have a station mistress. The lady concerned was Miss Margaret Elsden, the sister of Mr A.H. Elsden who eventually became station master at Birmingham Snow Hill; Miss Elsden later married Frank Buckingham who became station master at Oxford. Sadly, Wolvercot Platform was closed in January 1916 after a life of just eight years.

Wolvercot Siding Box survived the closure of Wolvercot Platform, and the 29-lever hip-roofed box controlled a level crossing giving vehicular access to adjacent meadows; the down starter at Wolvercot Siding carried the distant arms for Wolvercot Junction, just half a mile further on.

Wolvercot Junction was a place of some importance, for here the Oxford Worcester & Wolverhampton route diverged north-westwards from the Birmingham main line. The attendant signal box was a standard hipped-roof structure, controlling both main lines and the up and down goods loops which ended at this point. The box was a brick and timber structure containing a 35-lever frame. It is interesting to note that Wolvercot was both a railway junction *and* a canal junction, for here the Fourth Duke of Marlborough's connecting waterway left the Oxford Canal and, passing beneath the railway, headed westwards to join the River Thames. Opened in 1789, 'Duke's Cut' was a valuable link for narrow boats passing from the canal system to the Upper Thames, and in later years it became the main southern exit for pleasure craft leaving the Oxford Canal.

Gaining the Birmingham main line, Woodstock trains headed due north across a slightly unkempt area, dotted with scrubland, sheds and small allotments; ahead, an overbridge carried the ex-L & NWR 'Yarnton Loop' across the main line. A product of the 'Railway Mania', this short connection ran from the Bletchley line at Oxford Road Junction to the OW & WR at Yarnton, and was used primarily for freight traffic. An intriguing feature of this otherwise uninteresting area were the old Oxford horse trams which found a final resting place in surrounding farms and orchards. These had been purchased for use as bungalows and chalets following the closure of Oxford Tramways in 1914, but many were later broken up (the last survivor was moved from Paternoster Farm in the 1960s).

Northwards, the line passed beneath the A34 road, and then crossed Yarnton Lane on the level; a second level crossing, less than half a mile beyond, carried Sandy Lane across the line. With Kidlington village now visible over to the right, Woodstock trains rattled across the Oxford Canal on a skew bridge, beyond which a third level crossing was provided for the benefit of farmers using Roundham Lane. This was not a metalled road but level-crossing gates were provided, and there was a full-time gatekeeper in the person of Mr Ernest Goodwin, who lived in a cottage beside the line. Mr Goodwin started work with the GWR in 1913 and was originally in the engineering department, engaged in bridge construction and similar activities. In the 1920s he helped to install the new marshalling yards at Morris Cowley, but in 1938 he was involved in an accident and lost his right arm; after leaving hospital he was given the job of gatekeeper at Kidlington — a task he was to perform for the next 28 years. The crossing-keeper's house was typical of others erected on the Oxford & Rugby line during the 1870s; built of local stone, it was a gabled structure with a low-pitched slated roof. Mr and Mrs Goodwin had no gas or electricity, and all cooking was done on a coal-fired range. At night the cottage was lit by oil lamps.

With the Oxford Canal running more or less parallel to the left and the A423 converging from the right, trains approached Kidlington station (and the start of the Woodstock branch proper). Situated 5 miles 55 chains from Oxford, this small station had several unusual features. When opened in 1855, it had been a conventional two-platform stopping place, with a small yard and run-round loop for goods traffic on the down side. It is likely that two sidings were originally provided, one of which served a loading dock behind the down platform while the other passed through a typical Brunelian goods shed; there was also a short spur or headshunt at the northern end of the loop.

Towards the end of the 19th century a timber yard was opened on land to the west of the station and the goods shed siding was extended across the station approach in order to reach these new premises. This was hardly an ideal means of providing rail access because the lengthened goods siding cut across the station approach road in a very inconvenient way, and, when the siding was being shunted, potential travellers could not reach the ticket office! Even worse was the fact that wagons being unloaded in the goods shed blocked all means of entry to the timber yard. To overcome this problem it seems that an additional siding was installed to provide a 'bypass' for the goods shed and this effectively placed the shed

The main, down side station buildings at Kidlington were of typical Brunelian appearance; the valancing is, however, a later addition. This photograph is thought to date from around 1913. *British Railways*

on a short loop (see plans). As a result of these complicated alterations, Kidlington goods yard impinged on the station approach road to an unusual degree, and the problem was accentuated in 1923 when Oxford Farmers Ltd opened their bacon factory and a second siding was laid across the road.

A less obvious peculiarity of the station concerned its buildings, which were on the 'wrong' side of the railway. By convention station buildings were usually sited on the platform nearest the town or villages that they purported to serve, but Kidlington was to the east of the railway whereas its main station building and goods yard were on the western side; in effect the station was back-to-front! However, if we remember that Kidlington was opened to serve not Kidlington but Woodstock, this apparent mystery is solved — in 1855 Kidlington was merely a small village clustered round its church a mile or so to the east; such a tiny place did not need a station, and the station facilities were therefore placed on the *Woodstock* side of the line, at the end of Langford Lane. In the 1930s extensive ribbon development extended Kidlington west and northwards towards the railway, though the station remained poorly-sited in relation to the centre of the village and for this reason it was never particularly popular with villagers, who preferred the more convenient bus services to Oxford.

Kidlington's original track layout was left virtually unaltered when the station became a junction, the one significant addition to its infrastructure being a new terminal bay platform which was constructed on the alignment of a former goods siding. To allow sufficient room for terminating branch services, Kidlington's down platform was extended north towards the Banbury Road bridge, but the resulting arrangements were far from satisfactory insofar as there was insufficient room for a run-round loop. In consequence trains had to reverse out of their bay to run-round in a re-sited goods loop beyond the bridge, though this problem did not occur after the introduction of railmotors and auto-trains.

Architecturally, Kidlington was of great interest; its Cotswold stone station buildings were fully in the Brunelian tradition and, although it had unusual architectural details, its ground plan resembled scores of others erected all over the broad gauge system in the 1850s. It should be stressed that by the 1850s Brunel had to some extent tired of railway work and was concentrating more and more on his maritime activities; in a letter written to the architect Digby Wyatt he went so far as to claim that 'in detail of ornamentation I have no time or knowledge'. In later years, Brunel was content to delegate authority to his team of trusted assistants such as Robert Varden, William Gravatt and R.P. Brereton, any of whom could have been responsible for the building of Kidlington. There are, however, common design features on all Brunelian lines, suggesting that one person did indeed have overall control of each project, and it seems plausible, therefore, to describe Kidlington as a 'Brunel-type' station even though he may not have personally supervised its construction.

Built in 1855, Kidlington was one of a group of at least six stations erected at that time (the others being Heyford, Aynho, Box, St Clears and Clynderwen). Superficially, these six stations were a one-off batch, but on closer examination they were standard broad gauge stations with 'Cotswold' as opposed to 'Italianate' features. Kidlington was, for example, a mirror image of St Germans on the Cornwall Railway, but its hipped roof and larger canopy made it appear totally different.

Viewed from the platform, a traveller at Kidlington saw in front of him an asymmetrical façade with a deeply-recessed central section. The left-hand end of the building contained a commodious waiting room, with an attractive bay window giving a good view of oncoming trains. The recessed portion was the booking hall, and to the right were offices for the station master and booking office staff. The right-hand extremity of the building contained a porter's room and the gents' WC. A porch at the rear gave access to the booking hall, and three tall, Italianate chimneys projected through the roof; two of these served fireplaces in the main internal walls, while the third rose from a fireplace at the back of the ticket office. The booking hall was illuminated by a triple window in its rear wall, and this gave ample light in what would otherwise have been a rather gloomy interior. The building was constructed of local oolitic limestone, laid in regular courses, with ashlar work around the doors, windows and at the corners; there was also an ashlar string course about six feet from the ground. Projecting horizontal girders supported a large, all-round canopy, and the ends of each girder were decorated by cast 'lions' heads. In later years, the canopy was edged with typical Great Western 'V-and-hole' valancing.

A similar, but much smaller building on the up platform contained a ladies' waiting room and separate ladies' toilets, though, by analogy with other Brunelian stations, these facilities may have originally been intended for the use of first class travellers only.

Other structures at Kidlington included a characteristic broad gauge type goods shed and a standard Great Western covered footbridge. The goods shed was constructed of yellowish brickwork rather than the usual stone, suggesting that it may have been added after the opening of the station (though this 'Brunelian' design is unlikely to have appeared much later than the 1860s). The footbridge was much later, and was probably added at the turn-of-the-century when such structures were being mass-produced by the GWR for its 'cut-off' lines. Kidlington's 'classic' broad gauge style shed had five bays with prominent brick pilasters; its dimensions were approximately 57 ft × 40 ft. The gable ends were partially built of vertical timber planks, and featured separate entrances for road and railway vehicles. There was a central transhipment platform and a 1 ton 10 cwt hand-worked crane for lifting goods from road to rail. An office projected from the north wall, and the side wall contained three windows; as usual in 'Brunelian' goods sheds the main gable entrances had arched semi-circular openings.

The identity of Kidlington's earliest station masters is not known, but in the 1890s, and indeed for many years thereafter, William Cooke held sway over his half dozen staff. A slightly forbidding figure with a large walrus moustache, he lived in a house behind the up platform from which he could keep a close watch on his station; this personal supervision seems to have produced some attractive floral displays which, in season, enlivened both platforms at Kidlington. Climbing plants seem to have been Mr Cooke's speciality, and over the years a variety of exotic creepers appeared at the station, their tendrils clinging tenaciously to walls, lamp posts and to an

Kidlington station, looking northward from a convenient signal post during the Edwardian era. *British Railways*

The elaborate trellis structure on Kidlington's up platform. These adornments are thought to date from the Edwardian period, when station master William Cooke took a great interest in the station garden. *British Railways*

A general view of the down platform at Kidlington.

British Railways

elaborate trellis structure on the up platform. At a time in which most country stations had their own flower gardens, Kidlington railwaymen clearly decided to beat their rivals in the regular 'best kept station' competitions, and the *Great Western Magazine* contains several references to the station garden. In January 1911, for example, there is mention of a £5 special prize awarded to Kidlington, followed by a similar award in 1913.

William Cooke was replaced, in the late 1920s, by Harry Lloyd Pinnock, who for a time also supervised the terminus at Blenheim & Woodstock; Mr Pinnock's successors were John Elliott Jones and Jesse Silman — both of whom were responsible for Woodstock in addition to their duties at Kidlington. In 1940, however, growing wartime traffic (much of which was generated by the neighbouring RAF airfield) ensured that the two stations were once again given their own station masters, and Jesse Silman was relieved of his duties at Blenheim & Woodstock in order that he could have sole charge of the junction. Mr Silman remained at Kidlington throughout the war years, but by 1947 he had been replaced by Frederick Needle.

Other staff at Kidlington included porter Bill Coggins, signalman Gilbert Holder and signalman Frank Wise; in later years Mr Wise became a local councillor and after his death the nearby Railway Hotel was punningly named 'The Wise Alderman' in tribute to his work. Another Kidlington signalman, prior to 1916, had been Fred Badnell who, as a result of ill-health, was forced to retire prematurely; he finished his career as a gate-keeper at Stretton Road Crossing on the Shipston-on-Stour branch. Such changes were by no means uncommon, and although some men were content to remain in one place for several years, other (perhaps more ambitious) employees tended to move from station to station in pursuit of advancement. In 1912, for instance, signal porter R. Moulton moved to Wheatley as a full signalman, while in the following year lad porter Hazell was transferred to Mortimer. Another lad porter, Mr J.E. Jones, came to work at Kidlington in 1908 and retired from BR in 1960 after a

Driver Bill Pomeroy (left) and station master William Cooke (right) stand beside *Fair Rosamund* in the bay platform at Kidlington.
W. L. Kenning, cty. Adrian Vaughan

A general view of Kidlington, looking north towards Banbury in the British Railways period. The road bridge behind the station was rebuilt in 1923, and the concrete lamp posts were erected in 1931 when the platform lighting was converted from oil to paraffin vapour. In 1935 this station handled 22,559 passengers, 7,557 tons of goods and 14,250 parcels. The staff included 1 station master, 1 booking clerk, 2 porters, 3 signalmen and 5 crossing keepers.

Dr. G. D. Parkes

lifetime of service on the railway, in which he had risen 'through the ranks' to become station master at Thame.

The Blenheim & Woodstock branch was linked to the main line by a scissors crossover at the north end of Kidlington's down platform and, as mentioned earlier, it was possible in times of heavy traffic, for main line trains to be shunted onto the branch in order that more important workings could pass. This meant that in effect the branch was occupied by the shunted train, and to prevent accidents on the single line, an occupation key was provided at Kidlington. When the Blenheim & Woodstock branch was open for traffic, the key could be removed from its box if the Kidlington signalman sent a 'release staff for shunting signal' to Woodstock; the tappers on both the Woodstock and Kidlington electric train staff instruments were then held down simultaneously while the key was released. As an added precaution, lever collars were placed on the 'down main to branch home' and 'up branch home' signal levers in Kidlington box. When the branch was closed for traffic after the cessation of the day's train service, the occupation key remained out of its box so that main line trains could be refuged on the branch during the night and on Sundays. (These arrangements did not apply in later years, when the addition of a further crossover turned the southernmost extremity of the branch into a running loop controlled from Kidlington box.)

Leaving Kidlington, Woodstock trains passed beneath the A423 bridge and immediately swung leftwards onto their own line. Entering a cutting, the route continued due north, with a short run-round loop for goods traffic on the left and Kidlington Signal Box to the right. A small, brick and timber gabled structure, Kidlington box was in use by 1890 and replaced an earlier box that had been sited on the down platform. The new box originally had 51 levers including 13 spares, but in Colonel Yorke's inspection report of 1900, the box is said to contain only 46 levers.

Northwards, the three lines passed beneath a typical Brunel-designed overbridge, with three elliptical arches; the widely-spaced up and down main lines swept through the large central arch while the Woodstock line made use of a smaller arch to the left. The third arch, on the far side of the line, spanned a refuge siding with accommodation for 58-wagon freight trains.

Emerging from the cutting, trains accelerated through gently rolling countryside and soon reached a stretch of embankment with good views of the Oxford Canal, which was visible across fields to the left; the grey stone canal village of Thrupp could be seen strung out along the waterway, with brightly-coloured narrow boats and pleasure craft moored stem to stern beside the towpath.

Although rapidly eclipsed by the railway, working narrow boats used the Oxford Canal until the 1950s, and in World War Two a new concrete wharf was opened between Kidlington and Thrupp so that supplies for Kidlington aerodrome could be brought in by water transport. In the late 1940s and early 1950s the canal 'tankers' *Tweed* and *Rea* were among the last trading boats on the southern Oxford Canal. Owned by Thomas Clayton Ltd of Oldbury, they were crewed by Mr and Mrs Albert Beechey and carried gas tar from Oxford Gasworks to distilleries in the Midlands. Another Clayton's pair, at work around 1950, included the *Umea* and *Orwell*; these two 'gas boats' later replaced the *Tweed* and *Rea* on the Oxford run.

A crossover, situated 42 chains from Kidlington, connected the branch with the down main line, thus forming a down running loop with accommodation for 67 short wheelbase wagons; northwards, however, there was no further connection between main line and branch — though the three lines continued side by side for another half mile.

At Thrupp, trains crossed a small accommodation bridge with a span of 12 ft, and then rumbled over a much larger twin-span girder bridge carrying the triple-tracked line across the Cherwell. Continuing northwards, the railway was carried on a further stretch of embankment which was pierced, at one point, by another small accommodation bridge with a span of just 11 ft. To the left, travellers were rewarded with a good view of the canal which came within

'County' class 4–4–0 No. 3806 *County Kildare* pauses alongside the down platform at Kidlington while No. 1473 *Fair Rosamund* waits in the branch bay platform. The period is c.1930. *Lens of Sutton*

The branch auto-train in the down bay at Kidlington in the BR period; the 'Railway Hotel' visible in the background was subsequently renamed 'The Wise Alderman' in commemoration of Mr. Frank Wise, a former Kidlington signalman and councillor. *W. A. Camwell*

A through train from Woodstock to Oxford crossing from the branch to the up main at Kidlington; the new road overbridge can be seen to advantage in this post-war view. *Dr. G. D. Parkes*

yards of the railway before turning through 90 degrees at the west end of Thrupp village. Thereafter the waterway broadened and deepened to form 'Thrupp Wide', a popular spot with local artists and fishermen.

To the right, meanwhile, the view was a scene of pastoral tranquility, with tree-dotted meadows extending eastwards towards the deserted medieval village of Hampton Gay. On summer evenings, when a low sun cast long shadows across the grass, the overgrown foundations of this abandoned village could be clearly seen, together with acres of curious 'corrugations' in the surrounding fields which delineated the position of medieval plough lands.

More obvious to the casual observer was the lonely church of St Giles, standing in an isolated position in a field beside the railway; beyond, eagle-eyed travellers might have discerned the romantic, gabled ruins of Hampton Gay Manor, mysteriously burned down in 1887. An attractive spot in many ways, Hampton Gay was the scene of the worst accident in Great Western history, and, although this tragic event is peripheral to the Woodstock branch proper, it is clearly an integral part of the railway history of Kidlington. The story is, therefore, worth telling in some detail.

Christmas Eve 1874 was a cold, snowy day, yet the railways were crowded with people travelling home for Christmas. The 10 am Paddington to Birkenhead express was already packed when it arrived in Oxford at 12.06 pm and the station master, William Gibbs, added an ancient 4-wheeled coach to the front of the 14-coach train, presumably to accommodate extra travellers. This additional vehicle was coupled to the engine by its central screw coupling, but, unusually, the side chains were not used. The heavily-loaded narrow gauge express left Oxford at 12.15 pm, packed with 400 to 500 travellers, all of whom were no doubt looking forward to spending Christmas with their families in the Midlands. The northbound train was double-headed by Armstrong single wheelers Nos 478 (train engine) and 386 (pilot).

In an attempt to regain lost time, the 7 ft engines were driven flat out, and the express thundered through Woodstock Road (i.e. Kidlington) at about 40 miles per hour. Still accelerating, the train approached Hampton Gay, but unfortunately the leading right-hand wheel of the old 4-wheeled coach had started to disintegrate in the vicinity of Thrupp, and, glancing backwards, driver Harry Richardson on No 478 was startled by the sight of ballast and snow hurtling from beneath his train; fireman James Hill noticed a passenger leaning from the first coach and gesticulating for the train to stop. Instinctively, driver Richardson sounded his alarm whistle and both engines were thrown into reverse before the guard, William Price, could apply his own brakes. Sandwiched between two locomotives and a heavy train, the leading 4-wheeled vehicle immediately overturned, its splintered remains swerving down the embankment towards the frozen canal. Nine more of the coaches followed the 4-wheeler to destruction, but the two engines continued across the bridge unharmed. At least one packed passenger vehicle plunged into the canal, drowning some of its occupants. 'The cries and shrieks of the dying and injured', reported the *Oxford Times*, 'the ghastly silent dead, the fragments of human bodies and blood-stained clothing, and the prayers of those who discovered they had escaped serious injury rendered the scene one of indescribable horror. One poor man was quite delirious with an injury to the head and employed himself in preaching to the engine.'

Fortunately, help was at hand, and men from Hampton Gay paper mill, hearing the appalling noise of the crash, came running across the intervening fields to help the trapped and injured. Simultaneously, Mr Hallam, an Oxford surgeon who had been at nearby Shipton Manor, came hurrying across the frozen meadows from the opposite side of the line; other helpers included Lord Randolph Churchill and a party from Blenheim Palace. Meanwhile, William Butler, the driver of No 386, had driven full speed to Kirtlington station in order to stop up traffic, while uninjured passengers ran back to Woodstock Road to summon assistance and prevent down trains from ploughing into the wreck. Unfortunately, the telegraph wires were damaged and news of the disaster did not reach Oxford until 1.15 pm. However a rescue train arrived on the scene by 2.00 pm and the injured and uninjured travellers were soon back at Oxford.

Four of the injured died before reaching hospital and another four died later, bringing the death toll to 34 in this, the worst disaster in Great Western history. The dead included Richard Cartwright of Launton, Edward Sylvester of Oxford, Samuel Busbridge of Witney and 19-year-old Benjamin Taylor of Wolverhampton (whose grave can still be seen in Hampton Gay churchyard).

Over 100 were injured, including about 60 whose injuries could be described as serious. Meanwhile the tracks were still blocked at Hampton Gay and the police had difficulty in controlling vast crowds of sightseers on Christmas Day and Boxing Day. Both the *Oxford Times* and *Jackson's Oxford Journal* covered the disaster story in great detail, and the eye-witness account of the *Journal* reporter is worth quoting in full:–

'The third class carriage was smashed to atoms in a meadow, some 16 to 20 feet below . . . other carriages imitated with fatal precision the example set by the third class. One laid beyond it, wheels upward, and splintered into matchwood, parts of the fragments flying into the canal, whilst another, which had carried away the stone parapet of the bridge had evidently glanced over the top of the woodwork and plunged to the foot of the embankment, and was so completely ruined that the roof and lamps lay mixed up with the wheels and bottom of the carriage in dire confusion. Two other carriages lay next, on their side, both of course greatly shattered, and the next was a first class carriage which had found its way across the up line and was pitched down the embankment, and then three other carriages on the down side of the line, all lying on their side. One end of the first class was crumpled up, and the ghastly stains of blood on the yellow roof, the cushions and the floor testify to the terrible tragedy which was enacted therein. The engine and three or four carriages remained on the metals, and went some distance before they could be stopped . . . So utterly complete was the ruin of some of the carriages that the first thought which strikes the mind is, not that there were so many killed outright but so few, considering the large number that were on the train . . . underneath the carriage which laid wheels upwards, no less than 13 dead bodies were removed, all shockingly mutilated. Rushing as it did with irresistable force down the embankment the carriage seemed to have been ground to atoms as it crashed on the earth . . . there can be little doubt that the unfortunate occupants were hurried into eternity. The ground was thickly strewn with wood splinters, springs, lamps, glass, iron bars and bolts. The small fragments that remained of the faulty carriage laid high on the embankment. In the hollow beneath, the axle tree was to be observed, one wheel resting on the ground the other, that on which the tyre parted, being half buried in the clay.'

It is interesting to note that the *Oxford Journal* reporter immediately identified a broken tyre as the cause of the crash. Lord Randolph Churchill, who had spoken to the train crew at the scene of the accident, was also in no doubt that a

'14XX' 0–4–2T No. 1442 on 23rd March 1953, propelling the branch auto-train past Hampton Gay church, and the site of the 1874 train crash. *Dr. G. D. Parkes*

The Oxford Canal at Shipton-on-Cherwell. The bridge in the foreground carried a farm track across the waterway, while the substantial overbridge seen in the distance carried the Woodstock branch over the canal.

Packer Collection, Oxfordshire Museum Services, Woodstock

broken tyre had initiated the disaster, and on Christmas Day he wrote a remarkably accurate letter to the *Times* in which he argued that railway directors should be compelled by Parliament to provide 'powerful continuous brakes . . . to all express trains'.

Colonel Yolland of the Board of Trade was critical of the GWR in his report on the disaster. He found that the tyres of ex-Newport, Abergavenny & Hereford third class coach No 845 had been attached to the wheels by four countersunk rivets through the rims, and, though the company had agreed to abandon this form of construction, the offending vehicle had been repaired in such a way as recently as the 1860s. Furthermore, there had been no efficient means of communication between the drivers, passengers and guard, the Harrison communication cord fitted to the train having failed to work. In addition Colonel Yolland criticised the make-up of the train, and its insufficient brake power; 24th December 1874 had indeed been a black day for the Great Western Railway.

Not surprisingly, local superstition soon hinted that Hampton Gay was an evil spot, and the idea of some form of curse took even deeper root when the Manor House burned down on 29th April 1887. People recalled that the dead and dying had been carried to the house, and that the adjoining paper mill had been pressed into service as a temporary morgue. After the crash, it was said that Robert Pearson, the occupant of the old manor, had been so unnerved by what had happened that he gave up his tenancy and moved away. The manor was said to be haunted, and some local people would not visit its ruins — certainly not after dark! (As recently as 1984 a nearby council house tenant claimed that the ghost of 'a Victorian lady in a black dress' had appeared in his bedroom.)

Leaving the site of the 1874 tragedy, Woodstock trains crossed the winding River Cherwell on a substantial twin-span girder bridge, and immediately diverged north-westwards from the accompanying main line. The branch then followed its own curving embankment towards the Oxford Canal. To the right, the main line crossed the waterway on its own girder bridge, while dead ahead a tall, smoking chimney stack marked the presence of Shipton Cement Works. The canal bridge had two spans; a girder section carried the single line across the waterway and its towpath, and a brick arch spanned a nearby bridleway. Beyond, trains ran on a further stretch of embankment before entering a relatively deep cutting.

Climbing at 1 in 92, the branch headed due west for a short distance, with Shipton village to the left and the cement works in a deep hollow to the right. A private road belonging to the cement company was carried across the line on a skew bridge of brick and girder construction, after which the route turned sharply to the right and emerged on to a lofty embankment, giving travellers a good view of Shipton Cement Works and its extensive internal railway system.

In common with other industrial systems, the cement railway was worked by a diverse collection of 0–4–0 and 0–6–0 tank engines, some of which were of considerable

A close-up view of the Oxford Canal bridge seen in the previous photograph, with a '54XX' 0–6–0PT No. 5413 and a 70 ft auto-car.
Dr. G. D. Parkes

Above: An evocative shot of Collett 0–4–2T No. 1420 near Shipton-on-Cherwell Halt. The cement workers' houses at 'Bunkers Hill' are hidden behind the auto-coach; cement workers were the main source of traffic at this otherwise remote spot. The 1 in 69 gradient on the approach from Kidlington 'up Bunker Hill' is recalled as 'tricky with a mixed train', particularly on frosty mornings. *Dr. G. D. Parkes*

Having left the main line at Shipton-on-Cherwell, branch trains entered a cutting which was spanned by a brick and girder skew bridge, carrying a lane between Shipton village and Bunkers Hill. In later years this became a private road serving the cement works. *R. M. Casserley*

antiquity. The 'pride of the line' was perhaps No 5 *Westminster*, a Peckett 0–6–0 saddle tank, dating from 1917 and once used on the Fovant Military Railway in Wiltshire; this engine could be distinguished from a distance by its shining brass dome. The 0–4–0STs were of more conventional appearance; No 6 *C.F.S.*, for example, was a 26-ton industrial shunter built by Robert Stephenson & Hawthorn of Newcastle. All of the works engines were painted in a light green livery which did not show the ever-present cement dust.

The cement railway had its own reception loop and exchange sidings alongside the main line, in addition to the quarry system proper; the exchange sidings were a permanent installation, the connection to the main line being controlled by a standard Great Western gabled signal box which could be switched out when traffic was not being exchanged. The quarry sidings, in contrast, were composed of temporary flat-bottomed trackwork that could be shifted and slewed as quarrying proceeded. A 'main line' ran from the works to the quarry face and most of the works engines spent their time shuttling back and forth between the excavations and the works. Another engine would, meanwhile, be shunting loaded cement wagons in the exchange sidings (main line locomotives were not allowed to pass a stop board at the entrance to the works).

In addition to its locomotives, the cement works employed two steam navvies until electric excavating machinery was introduced in the 1930s (thereafter one of the steam navvies

was retained as a spare). A small engine shed was provided near the exchange sidings, but the works shunters were usually berthed in the open at the cessation of each day's quarrying. Maintenance work was carried out 'on site', and the servicing area was invariably littered with connecting rods, saddle tanks and other bits of dismantled locomotives!

When first opened, the quarry had been relatively small, but, as more and more material was excavated, its size inexorably increased until eventually the triangular wedge of land between the branch and the main line became one great hole in the ground. From their trains, Woodstock branch travellers could see the quarry spread out below them, the cement works' engines looking like models. In the distance, the red brick cement workers' houses at Bunkers Hill could be clearly seen, while in the foreground a quarry wagon stood mysteriously isolated on a short length of track.

Following its great curving embankment, the route climbed slightly at 1 in 69 as it crossed the A423 Banbury Road on a steel girder bridge; beyond, the railway dipped towards Shipton-on-Cherwell Halt. This sleeper-built stopping place was 2 miles 9 chains from Kidlington, and sited on the up side of the line. A simple wooden shelter was provided for the convenience of waiting travellers, and at night the halt was illuminated by two wooden lamp posts which supported traditional glass lanterns with ornamental finials. A similar lamp post stood at the bottom of the embankment, where a 'kissing gate' gave access to the sloping cinder path that ascended to rail level. The glass lanterns held simple oil lamps which were lighted and trimmed by the guards of passing trains.

It is interesting to find that when built, in the early months of 1929, Shipton-on-Cherwell Halt cost only £160. Unfortunately it had been constructed on the lines of a railmotor halt with a very low platform, and in 1933 the Great Western was obliged to spend a further £120 on raising it to standard height. Shipton had a single wooden nameboard at platform level, and an additional name board stood on the north side of the embankment facing the road; this proclaimed in large letters 'SHIPTON-ON-CHERWELL HALT FOR TRAINS TO BLENHEIM OXFORD BANBURY ETC'.

As their trains paused briefly at Shipton, inquisitive American travellers may have wondered why the nearby cement workers' houses stood in an area known as 'Bunkers Hill'; did this commemorate the defeat inflicted on their rebellious ancestors in 1775? (An adjoining area on the north side of the quarry was known as 'Gibraltar', and inevitably, a nearby canalside inn was punningly called 'The Rock of Gibraltar'!)

Leaving Shipton-on-Cherwell, the branch headed westwards through rolling countryside, with open fields to the south and wooded land to the north. Still on an embankment the route climbed gently at 1 in 129 towards Woodstock, crossing a farm track on a steel girder bridge with a single span of 22 ft; a glance to the left revealed two attractive

'54XX' 0–6–0PT No. 5413 running through the deep cutting between Shipton and Woodstock; the gentle grading of the sides is probably evidence of the generous excavation to provide spoil for use elsewhere on the line. With the prospect of a long lay-over at Woodstock between afternoon trips, one fireman recalls being dropped off and left in the cutting on the way in for the purpose of cutting beansticks. This highly unofficial practice passed the time and resulted in some impressive bundles collected on the last trip (empty stock) and taken back to Oxford shed in the depleted bunker. No doubt the sight of a Woodstock crew strolling out of the shed with such trophies was the envy of less fortunate men, weary after a more arduous duty. Woodstock fixed distant can be seen to the right. *R. H. G. Simpson*

Cotswold stone houses, while to the right Slade Farm was partially hidden by a belt of trees. Continuing through this pleasant, elm-dotted landscape, the line entered a cutting, and with startled rabbits scurrying away on either side, trains passed beneath an arched brick overbridge. Beyond, the route continued westwards through the cutting, which, like the Shipton canal bridge, was wide enough to accommodate a double track.

Passing a sleeper-built platelayer's hut and the Woodstock fixed distant, the auto-trains then rumbled beneath a second brick overbridge at the end of the cutting. Similar small huts were provided at intervals along the line, examples being at Woodstock, Shipton-on-Cherwell, Hampton Gay and at Kidlington. Built to the same basic design, they had a window in the front and a brick-built chimney stack at the rear. A side door opened onto a small vestibule with rows of coat pegs on which the permanent way men could hang their oilskins and greatcoats before entering the dark but snug interior of the hut, where in wet or cold weather a roaring fire provided warmth between spells of work on the track.

Emerging from its cutting, the railway curved towards the south-west and approached Woodstock on a final stretch of embankment. With a minor road running parallel to the right, the line crossed another girder bridge and entered its terminus. Trains clattered past a lineside timber yard and J & R Pullman's glove factory before entering the single passenger platform at Blenheim & Woodstock station. Slowing to walking pace, the branch train finally came to rest beside the Cotswold stone terminal buildings, 9 miles 32 chains from Oxford and 3 miles 57 chains from the bay platform at Kidlington.

Built on a former medieval burgage plot, the station buildings occupied a narrow gap between cottages and the Church of England school, but happily the 'L'-shaped booking offices and waiting rooms blended favourably with surrounding buildings. Limited space meant that the main goods entrance was situated in Hensington Road, though a small gate beside the passenger buildings gave access to the adjacent end-loading dock.

Like Kidlington, Blenheim & Woodstock station was built of local, honey-coloured stone, again laid in regular courses, with ashlar quoins and window surrounds. The main block faced Oxford Road, in which position it was almost opposite the 'Hensington Gates' of Blenheim Park — which were often used on ceremonial occasions. Perhaps for this reason, the station was given a more or less symmetrical façade, with a slightly recessed central portion and two projecting 'pavilions'. Sir John Vanbrugh's monumental Baroque style was hardly

A Woodstock to Oxford through train rumbling through the cutting between Woodstock and Shipton, with Harry Collins in control from the trailer; the locomotive was 0–6–0PT No. 5413. *R. H. G. Simpson*

Woodstock station from the Oxford Road, showing (right) the main public entrance, (centre) the booking office door and (left) the double doors giving access to the parcels office.
W. A. Camwell

Two views of the main facade of Blenheim & Woodstock station in the early 1950s, showing useful detail of the canopy supports.
R. H. G. Simpson and J. H. Moss

Collett '14XX' class 0–4–2T No. 1446 and auto-coach No. 110 stand in the platform at Blenheim & Woodstock in July 1947. Although most branch trains ran more or less empty, significant numbers of people travelled to Oxford on market days, and some workings were literally packed with children travelling to the Sterling Cinema in Kidlington. Locomotives always ran at the Woodstock end of the train and this meant that when mixed trains were run from Woodstock to Kidlington, the formation was auto-coach + loco + wagon and 'Toad' brake van. *J. H. Russell*

fashionable in 1890, but in some ways the vaguely classical proportions of the Bodmin design used at Woodstock station echoed the nearby palace, and this was possibly the intention of the station's builders.

Entering Woodstock station from the road, the traveller would normally have walked through a set of double doors at the right-hand end of the building; these led into a small, fully-roofed circulating area from which one could emerge onto the platform or turn left into the booking office. Alternatively, one might have entered the booking office via a single door which opened directly onto the forecourt, but, as this door was usually kept shut, most travellers used the always-open double doors. A second pair of double doors was situated in the left-hand corner of the building and these gave access to a parcels room. A separate range contained various additional accommodation including ladies' and gentlemens' toilets, porters' rooms and the station master's office. As already mentioned, surviving plans of the station show a *wooden* building, of similar appearance to the stone structure that was eventually built; one assumes that this wooden building was rejected on the grounds that it was out of keeping with the historic nature of its surroundings.

The platform was covered by a projecting canopy, and there was a smaller canopy at the front of the building, sheltering the passenger entrances but not the parcels office. Both Woodstock and Kidlington stations were painted in the Great Western's usual light creamy-buff colour, with doors and other details picked out in a contrasting dark buff or brown colour. Old photographs show that at Woodstock, the 'brown' was very dark, and may have resembled the familiar Western Region 'chocolate' colour; in the Edwardian era the doors and window frames at Woodstock were painted in this dark buff colour, but a lighter shade was later applied.

Woodstock goods shed was hardly a picturesque specimen, being built entirely of corrugated iron. It is conceivable that when first planned, the Woodstock directors intended that small freight and sundries would be loaded and unloaded in a small platform alongside the passenger station, in which case the parcels office, with its large door, would have provided covered accommodation in lieu of a proper goods shed, leaving the goods yard for coal and wagon load traffic. The decision to provide a large goods shed in addition to the parcels unloading area may have been an afterthought — hence the appearance of a lightly-built corrugated-iron structure in an otherwise well-built terminus. Alternatively, the Woodstock Railway's budget may have been strained by the lavish passenger building with the result that the goods shed was built as cheaply as possible.

Built from standard pre-fabricated components, Woodstock goods shed had two windows in the south side and four on the north, together with a pair of sliding doors for road vehicles and hinged doors in each gable for rail traffic. The office, which extended from the eastern gable, resembled a standard round-topped hut, similar to others provided for use as offices, garages, hay stores and other purposes at smaller GW stations.

Woodstock's long-demolished engine shed had also been fabricated from standard corrugated-iron components, and plans suggest that when first built the shed measured 70 ft × 18 ft. It was a gabled structure, with a shallow clerestory along the apex of its roof, and an entrance for locomotives in the western end. When the terminus was remodelled

Detail of the terminal buffers at Blenheim & Woodstock, showing the small circulating area between the main terminal buildings and the subsidiary block. *Dr. G. D. Parkes*

Detail of the eastern end of the subsidiary block which housed the gentlemen's lavatories. Items of interest in this post-war view include the gas lamp with its World War Two blackout shade, and the station gardens which were well maintained until closure. *Dr. G. D. Parkes*

Woodstock in the summer of 1949. Station master Leslie Turner (in shirt-sleeves) is engaged in conversation with the guard. When a goods train was run the auto-trailer was left behind and stabled in the siding visible to the right. *J. H. Moss*

around 1899, the shed was shortened by 23 ft, leaving space for just one engine; at the same time the building was re-sited. There had originally been a simple wooden coaling platform, measuring 21½ ft × 12½ ft, but this structure was demolished in 1899 and not replaced. (Although Woodstock's iron goods shed was rare, corrugated-iron engine sheds were found at several other Great Western termini, notably at Newcastle Emlyn, where the small sub-shed was not unlike its counterpart at Woodstock, albeit with a round-topped roof. Elsewhere, the Cambrian Railways evolved a very similar corrugated-iron design, examples being found at Builth Wells and Llanfyllin.)

Unfortunately, there are no surviving photographs showing Blenheim & Woodstock signal box in its entirety, but there is sufficient information to enable a generalised picture to be built up. Like many other small Great Western boxes, it measured roughly 16 ft × 12 ft, and was of weather-boarded construction with a hipped, slated roof. Unusually, for so small a box, it was approximately three storeys high, this disproportionate height being needed to give signalmen a clear view over the adjacent water tower and engine shed. A tall stove-pipe chimney projected through the roof, and access to the upper storey was via a long flight of steps on the eastern side.

Other small structures were of a varied nature, and included a corrugated-iron lamp hut near the buffers, a stone-built weigh-house and a small coal office used by Marriotts' employees. Of these diverse structures, the weigh-house is the only one calling for further comment. A square building, it had a window at the front and a door in its west wall; the chimney had an unusual 'Italianate' cap, similar to those found at Kidlington, but much smaller. (Care and maintenance of the delicate weighing machinery was undertaken by Messrs H. Pooley & Sons, but the station master was responsible for balancing and adjusting the machine each morning and as necessary throughout the day.)

Finally, the water tower was constructed of red and blue bricks, laid in the usual 'English Bond' style with alternate courses of headers and stretchers. There were two arched window apertures in the south side but no doors or windows in the north wall; access to the open-topped metal tank was by means of an iron ladder, and there was a door to the lower storey in the east wall. This lower storey was initially used as a store room by the locomotive department, but in later years the bottom part of the tower became a general purpose store for platelayers' tools and other equipment. The iron tank, manufactured by Ransomes & Rapier of London, incorporated a swan-necked water crane for filling locomotives. A characteristic GW-style 'fire devil' stood beside the water crane; this was kept alight during periods of freezing weather, but failed to stop the formation of ice during the Arctic winter of 1947. Ex-fireman Frank Parsons recalled that the column was covered in icicles 'like a Christmas tree'. In summer, one or two daring individuals would swim in the open tank, which was alleged to contain prize fish!

In its last years, Woodstock had a staff of only four, but in earlier years, when the branch was fully signalled, the station had given employment to seven men. After 1926 the range of duties carried out by station staff was much reduced; shunting, for example, would be carried out by shunter guards such as Harry Wharton or Alf Kew, while the two

A useful view of the platform buildings, for all intents and purposes stone-built versions of a standard GWR design. The nearby Oxford Worcester & Wolverhampton Railway line stations at Kingham and Evesham were of similar appearance, albeit of brick construction.

J. H. Russell

'54XX' 0–6–0PT No. 5413 simmers beside the station buildings at Woodstock during a midday lay-over between services. As the station was so conveniently situated in the heart of town, crews would pass the time wandering round the shops or enjoying a haircut.

R. H. G. Simpson

A general view of the corrugated iron goods shed at Blenheim & Woodstock. Most loading and unloading took place in the 'main' goods siding, and in later years the short spur alongside the cattle dock was virtually disused. In its final years Woodstock goods yard handled about 8,000 tons of goods traffic a year, roughly half of this figure being coal traffic. In 1951 the station received 3,543 tons of coal and 1,034 tons of general merchandise, while outward traffic included 2,047 tons of stone or other minerals. The west ground frame covering can be seen alongside the release crossover. This feature was added in 1925 when Woodstock's signalling was simplified. The signalling history of the Woodstock branch can be divided into three distinct phases, that is to say, from 1890 until about 1899 when it was fully signalled but worked by train staff and ticket; from 1899 until 1925 when it was worked by electric train staff; and from 1925 until closure when the line reverted to ordinary train staff operation as a 'one-engine-in-steam' route.

J. H. Russell

Forecourt view of the goods shed, showing the projecting office with its curiously positioned and unused end door. The 1904 *Railway Clearing House Handbook of Stations* lists a 5 ton yard crane, but in later years there was only a 1 ton 10 cwt crane inside the goods shed. *J. H. Russell*

After World War Two (and probably also before it) the daily freight seldom exceeded half a dozen wagons, and shunting operations were usually carried out with the auto-trailer attached; indeed freight workings were generally worked in this way as it was not worth the bother of disconnecting the auto-gear to release the trailer. In this late 1940s view, auto-car No. 110 is seen projecting from the goods shed during shunting operations. *J. H. Russell*

'517' class 0–4–2T No. 1159 and auto-trailer No. 110 entering the goods yard at Woodstock during routine shunting operations. Apparently, this move had to be carried out with great care otherwise the ungainly trailer would develop a sway on the crossover, and the clearances through the goods shed were extremely tight, as seen in the previous view. The entrance to the goods yard (hidden behind the locomotive's cab) was tucked away in the residential Hensington Road, traditional space and pale gates closing across the head of the alley leading into the yard.
J. H. Russell

Regular shipments of leather for the glove factory arrived in vans and were unloaded in the goods shed. Frustratingly, few photographs discovered show anything of the edge of the goods yard, cattle pens, etc., but this view does at least feature the small hut used by James Marriott's employees as a coal office. *J. H. Russell*

ground frames would be operated by porters. When first opened, the post of station master at Blenheim & Woodstock had been a prestigious position, and Albert Lofting the town's first station master, was a figure of some importance, responsible not only for the day-to-day running of the station but also in charge on ceremonial occasions when royalty and other VIPs arrived by train. Mr Lofting was replaced by Thomas Ashford in the mid-1890s, and this sad-faced, slightly stooping man remained at Woodstock for the next three decades, in which time he became something of a local celebrity.

Like many other country station masters, Mr Ashford took an active part in local community activities, and it seems that one of his favourite part-time activities was the St John Ambulance Brigade. All GWR employees were encouraged to join this organisation, but at Blenheim & Woodstock the entire workforce was involved; perhaps they were attracted by the smart, military-style uniforms in use at the time, which certainly gave them an opportunity to participate in some of Blenheim's Edwardian pageantry. In 1906, for example, 'Sergeant' Ashford marched his staff up to the palace in grand style, the proceedings being reported as follows in the October 1906 *Great Western Magazine*:–

> 'The Woodstock Corps of the St John Ambulance Brigade paraded on August 8th, and marched to Blenheim Palace to receive at the hands of her Grace the Duchess of Marlborough awards gained during the session. Among those who had the honour of receiving presentations were several members of staff of the Blenheim & Woodstock station, including Messrs T. Ashford (Station Master), Hunt, Godman, Peare, Hine, Carwas and Bryant'.

Thomas Ashford retired around 1925, his career having spanned the branch's heyday. There was then something of a hiatus when, as part of its rationalisation plans, the Great Western placed both Woodstock and Kidlington under the control of one station master in the person of Harry Lloyd Pinnock. The idea may have been to demote the branch to such an extent that it did not have its own station master, but, as we have already seen, there was a reversion to the previous arrangements in World War Two when Jesse Silman (having initially been responsible for both stations) was replaced at Woodstock by Emlyn Davies. There was, thereafter, a succession of station masters including (in chronological order) Harry Bush, Aubrey Walker, Leslie Turner, and finally, Gilbert Ludlow.

Although the Eighth Duke of Marlborough had rapidly lost interest in the Woodstock Railway once it was fully operational, his earlier interest in the project *had* enabled the line to be brought right into the old town and, unlike many branch line stations, Blenheim & Woodstock was ideally situated within yards of the town centre. Leaving the platform, travellers walked through the terminal buildings and into Oxford Road, from where it was only a short stroll into the town's irregularly-shaped main street. Old Cotswold stone buildings could be seen on all sides, among them the Georgian Bear Hotel — once Woodstock's premier coaching

The Great Western 1890 General Powers Act stipulated that Woodstock station should be provided with 'all proper and sufficient station fittings' including a 'water tank and a water crane'. The tank erected by Lucas & Aird was provided by Ransomes & Rapier of London who may also have provided the swan-necked water crane, which was unlike any standard GW fitting. The brick base itself bore no evidence of GW architectural practice and may well have been built to drawings provided by Ransomes. Details of the original pumping arrangements have not come to light but from 1910 the tank was fed from mains supply. Latterly the brick base was used as a store room and its internal dimensions were officially quoted as 9 ft 9 in x 5 ft 9 in. The capacity of the tank was only 3,206 gallons.

J. H. Russell

This view of No. 1159 during shunting operations in the 1940s features the rear of the water tower. The engine shed and signal cabin which also occupied this area had long since been demolished. The small glove factory in the right distance was not served directly by any siding, though the adjacent goods headshunt has sometimes been mistakenly called a 'glove factory siding'. *J. H. Russell*

inn — and the 18th-century Town Hall. Blenheim Palace was situated to the west of the town, pedestrian access being, in the words of the *Little Guide to Oxfordshire*:–

> 'at the west end of the main street of the town, through a heavy triumphal arch, which the Duchess had erected the year after the (First) Duke's death, with a Latin inscription outside and a translation of it on the inside.'

Entry to the gardens was, in the 1930s, only 6d, but those wishing to visit the palace (Tuesdays, Wednesdays and Thursdays only) had to pay a much greater fee of 2s.

The palace itself was, for most of its life, a controversial structure, and only in modern times has its true grandeur gained critical acceptance. Writing in 1906. F.G. Brabant, the author of the *Little Guide*, clearly found it impossible to give more than grudging praise:–

> 'As to its architectural merits, opinions will probably always differ. To judge it fairly one should clear one's mind of the prejudice naturally created by the date of its erection . . . that the Palace is heavy and ungraceful its admirers will hardly deny, but it may lay claim to a massive dignity and a skilful combination of its parts.'

Quite apart from its obvious historical and architectural attractions, Blenheim was of interest to the railway enthusiast as the site of a little-known 3 ft gauge railway that was installed around 1896 when the Ninth Duke impulsively decided that his one-and-a-half mile long ornamental lake needed cleaning and dredging (he was overseas at the time). Contractors were called in, and in the next few months a temporary 3 ft gauge railway was laid around the lake in order that a small 0–4–0T known as *Jubilee* could haul away train loads of evil-smelling sludge. Little is known about this contractor's railway, though it is thought that *Jubilee* and her train of side-tipping wagons were delivered to Woodstock by train and then hauled through the town by horses.

An enlargement of the photograph shown on page 95 to provide a reasonably clear view of the small weigh house. The original weighing machine was replaced in 1938, because the existing 7 ton machine could not accommodate motor lorries. *C. L. Turner*

'54XX' class 0–6–0PT No. 5413 at Blenheim & Woodstock in 1954.

P. B. Whitehouse

CHAPTER SIX

THE BRITISH RAILWAYS PERIOD (1948–1954)

THE end of World War Two was followed by the return of a Labour Government, pledged to nationalise rail transport and other important industries, and on 31st December 1947 a nationwide fanfare of locomotive whistles heralded the birth of 'British Railways' and the end of private ownership. In many places a feeling of elation filled the air, but there were no special celebrations in Oxford or Woodstock. Indeed, the immediate effects of nationalisation were remarkably few, and life on the Woodstock branch went on much as before. The only obvious change concerned the liveries of locomotives and rolling stock — and even this modest innovation took many months to fully implement. The familiar chocolate and cream GW coach livery was replaced by a striking red and cream colour scheme which looked very smart on branch auto-trains. Locomotives, on the other hand, appeared in drab unlined black, and though, in theory, 'mixed traffic' engines should have appeared in L & NWR style lined-black livery, it seems that this scheme was rarely applied to smaller ex-GW tank engines.

Post-war train services were similar to those provided in the Great Western era, with a basic weekday pattern of 8 trains each way including the morning, evening and mid-day Oxford trips. In 1947/48 up trains left Woodstock at 7.58 am, 9.30 am, 12.22 pm, 12.58 pm, 3.50 pm, 5.22 pm, 6.20 pm and 7.10 pm, these times remaining virtually unchanged until closure.

Train Working in the Post-War Period

The Woodstock branch service was covered by two 8-hour shifts, involving four locomen. The early shift arrived for work

A post-war shot of No. 5413 at the terminus in 1949, a chalked smokebox number the only intimation of nationalisation. *J. H. Moss*

at Oxford shed at about 03.00 am and worked an empty stock trip to Kingham before returning to Oxford with an up OW & WR line stopping service. The same crew then travelled to Woodstock with the morning through train, arriving at 7.31 am. The first up service of the day left Woodstock at 7.58 am, picking up any incoming freight vehicles at Kidlington and shunting the bacon factory with the auto-trailer attached. The 08.40 am return service to Woodstock was a mixed working, a typical formation being the auto-trailer, followed by 3 or 4 wagons, a couple of vans and the 'Toad' brake van. This was a considerable load for an 0-4-2T, and if the rails were wet or greasy, the engine might slip on the sharp curve at Thrupp; on these occasions the fireman would have to jump down onto the ballast and sand the rails by hand (the sand pipes did not always align on curves). On arrival at Woodstock the train ran straight into the platform to allow any travellers to disembark, and then backed into the run-round loop prior to shunting the yard. As mentioned in Chapter 4, this would be done with the passenger trailer still coupled to the engine, which was quite feasible in view of the small number of goods vehicles involved (though, if the steps of the passenger trailer were accidentally left unfolded, they could catch on the goods shed doors and be torn off).

Having completed these modest shunting duties, the engine and trailer left Woodstock on a passenger working at 9.30 am, arriving in Kidlington eight minutes later. There was then a long 'gap' in the timetable in which the crew (who had been at work since 3.00 am) had their breakfast, sometimes

Guard Ned Giles, fireman Frank Parsons, and driver Harry Collins pose beside auto-car No. W58 at Kidlington in 1949.
J. H. Moss

KIDLINGTON and BLENHEIM & WOODSTOCK BRANCH.

AUTO CAR—ONE CLASS ONLY.

SINGLE LINE between Blenheim and Woodstock and Kidlington, worked by Train Staff and only one Engine in steam at a time, or two coupled together. No Block Telegraph on this Line. Form of Staff, Round; Colour Red.

Down Trains. **Week Days only.**

Distance M.	C.	STATIONS.	Ruling Gradient 1 in	B Oxford Auto.		B Auto Mixed.		B Auto.	K Freight SX		B Auto. ‡		B Oxford Auto.		B Auto.		G Engine and Van. K		B Auto.		B Auto.	
				a.m.		a.m.		a.m.	noon.		p.m.		p.m.		p.m.		p.m.		p.m.		p.m.	
—	—	**Kidlington** .... dep.	—	7 23	....	8 40	....	11 15	12 0	....	12 38	....	2 40	....	4 10	....	5† 5	....	5 38	....	6 52	....
2	9	**Shipton-on-Cherwell Halt** .. „	69 R	7 28	..	8 46	..	11 20	RR	..	12 43	..	2 45	..	4 15	..	—	..	5 43	..	6 57	..
3	57	**Blenheim & Woodstock** .. .... arr.	129 R	7 31	....	8 50	....	11 23	12 10	....	12 46	....	2 48	....	4 18	....	5†13	....	5 46	....	7 0	....

‡—May run as a Mixed trip when necessary at point-to-point times shewn for other Mixed trips. K—Suspended.

Up Trains. **Week Days only.**

STATIONS.	Ruling Gradient 1 in	B Auto Mixed.		B Auto.		G Engine and Van. SX	B Auto.		B Oxford Auto.			B Auto.		K Freight K		B Auto.		B Auto.		B Auto.	
		a.m.		a.m.		a.m.	p.m.		p.m.			p.m.		p.m.		p.m.		p.m.		p.m.	
Blenheim & Woodstock .. .... dep.	—	7 58	....	9 30	....	11†30	12 22	....	12 58	....	....	3 50	....	4 40	....	5 22	....	6 20	....	7 10	....
Shipton-on-Cherwell Halt .. „	129 F	8 2	..	9 33	..	RR	12 25	..	1 1	..	..	3 53	..	—	..	5 25	..	6 23	..	7 13	..
Kidlington .... arr.	69 F	8 8	....	9 38	....	11†38	12 30	....	1 6	....	....	3 58	....	4 50	....	5 30	....	6 28	....	7¶18	....

K—Suspended. ¶—Thence empty to Oxford at 7†25 p.m.

No. 1

293

The 1948 working timetable.

The Woodstock branch 'Toad' brake van on the main goods siding, where it was usually left overnight. The cattle dock and its short siding can only be glimpsed in the background. *Dr. G. D. Parkes*

frying eggs and bacon on a polished shovel placed just inside the firebox. At 11.15 am, engine and trailer returned to Woodstock; the next up working was a freight, and if there were reasonable numbers of wagons to be conveyed to Kidlington the auto-trailer would be detached and left in the carriage siding. Usually, however, there were few vehicles, other than an empty coal wagon or two, and the engine would therefore work its freight with the trailer still coupled-up. If any incoming vehicles had been deposited at Kidlington by the main line 'pick-up' goods, they would be worked back to Woodstock at 12 noon. Finally, at 12.58 pm, the 'early' crew returned to Oxford, arriving in the up main platform; the branch train would then cross to the down bay prior to forming the next service to Blenheim & Woodstock.

The 'late' (or afternoon) shift worked through to Woodstock with the afternoon train, arriving at 2.48 pm. As the next departure was not until 3.50 pm, there was time for a cup of tea and a chat with the station staff, or perhaps a stroll into the town. At 5.22 pm the branch train made a further return trip to Kidlington, followed by another round trip at 6.20 pm; the 5.38 pm from Kidlington back to Woodstock might carry senior school children from Oxford. There had traditionally been an afternoon freight working from Woodstock to Kidlington, but by the 1950s this ran only 'if required' and the daily timetable ended with a final up working to Kidlington at 7.10 pm, after which the locomotive and trailer ran empty stock to Oxford at 7.25 pm.

Locomotives and Rolling Stock 1947–1954

In its last years the line was worked mainly by Collett 0–4–2Ts (which, in 1946, were renumbered in the 14XX series to make room for newly-built oil-burning 2–8–0s). Several 14XXs appeared on the branch, including Nos 1420, 1442, 1448, 1450 and 1473. Another locomotive seen on the Woodstock line at this time was 54XX 0–6–0PT No 5413. Introduced in 1930/31, the 54XX class, with 5 ft 2 in wheels, was designed specifically for auto-train working, and was originally used mainly in the London area. The use of these six-coupled engines was appreciated by train crews, as the four-coupled 14XX class had never been entirely satisfactory for freight or shunting duties. Unfortunately, Oxford's allocation of small 'yellow' or 'uncoloured' tank locomotives was limited, and when the regular engines were not available 74XX panniers were occasionally used. These were very similar to the 54XX class but better for freight with their smaller 4 ft 7½ in wheels. They were not fitted for push-pull working and consequently they were not popular with train crews who had to run-round before and after every ten minute trip. Oxford-based 74XX 0–6–0PTs included Nos 7404, 7411 and 7412, and all three may have appeared on an irregular basis.

TYPICAL MOTIVE POWER ON THE WOODSTOCK BRANCH c.1900–1954

Class	*Wheelbase*	*Typical numbers*
517	0–4–2T	1159/1473/1478/1484
Metro *	2–4–0T	3585/3588/3589
1501 *	0–6–0PT	1531/1742
1901 *	0–6–0PT	1935
14XX	0–4–2T	1420/1442/1448/1450/1473
54XX	0–6–0PT	5413
74XX *	0–6–0PT	7404/7411/7412

* = Probably used when regular 517 or 14XX locos not available during overhauls, etc.

The Great Western's streamlined AEC railcars were designed specifically for use on certain lightly-used main line services, but they were eventually cascaded onto more lowly duties, and by the late 1940s several cars were in use on

No. 5413 at Blenheim & Woodstock while its crew eat their sandwich lunches in the station. *R. H. G. Simpson*

London Division branch lines. In July 1949 one of these vehicles was diagrammed for work on the Woodstock branch, but this interesting innovation was a result of overall timetable planning in the Oxford area, and was not intended to revolutionise efficiency on the Woodstock route.

Supplements to the London Division working timetable reveal that, after working through to Oxford at 12.58 pm, the 'Blenheim Auto' made a round trip to Princes Risborough. Meanwhile, a railcar worked the 2.30 pm Oxford to Woodstock, after which this same vehicle worked the 3.50 pm and 5.22 pm services to Kidlington, arriving at 3.58 pm and 5.30 pm respectively. At 5.55 pm the railcar returned to Oxford as an unadvertised through working, while at 4.42 pm the normal 14XX and trailer itself arrived from Oxford. Thereafter, the railcar spent the rest of the day working on the Princes Risborough line, while the 14XX resumed its normal duties shuttling back and forth between Woodstock and Kidlington. One result of the use of diesel traction on the branch was a suspension of the traditional mid-afternoon freight trip from Kidlington to Blenheim & Woodstock — which ceased to run in 1948 and was not reinstated when all branch services reverted to locomotive working.

Passenger vehicles seen in the final months exhibited as much variety as in pre-war years, and trailers used in the branch in the 1950s included Nos W87W, W183W and W185W; these were all venerable wooden-bodied vehicles dating from the Edwardian era, and all three looked their age. Like old canal boats, they tended to 'hog' longitudinally, and, when their glass toplights became hopelessly loose, BR was obliged to tack metal sheeting along the tops of each side. The cars were painted in red and cream livery after nationalisation, but this attractive livery was often marred by layers of grime; in her last years, 'Rosie' looked a sorry sight.

Closure of the Branch

It was clear that after World War Two the line was carrying very few passengers, and on many trips the trains ran with no passengers at all. In an attempt to remedy this situation Monty Turner (Woodstock's last-but-one station master) arranged some excursions to Oxford, but, in spite of posters, and extensive canvassing, few additional customers were attracted, and the experiment was abandoned after a few weeks. The only busy period came once a year when a large agricultural show was held on part of Kidlington aerodrome, and travellers would book to Shipton Halt and walk the short distance from there to the show ground. This brief period of heavy traffic could not sustain the branch for 52 weeks of the year, and by 1950 the writing was clearly 'on the wall' for the little-used Blenheim & Woodstock line.

Apart from Mr Turner's valiant (and unofficial) efforts, there had not, for many years, been any real attempt to tailor branch train services to the needs of local people, few of whom had any desire to travel from Woodstock to Kidlington or vice-versa. Kidlington, a large village of some 1,900 people, provided neither work nor significant shopping facilities and the only real attraction for Woodstock residents was perhaps the Sterling Cinema — though even this was a mile away from the station. Oxford was a major centre for shopping and employment, but, as we have seen, only a small proportion of branch trains worked through to that important destination, and it is perhaps unfortunate that Woodstock branch services could not have been integrated with other secondary services

KIDLINGTON and BLENHEIM & WOODSTOCK. (ONE CLASS ONLY. AUTO CAR—) **Week Days only.**

SINGLE LINE between Blenheim and Woodstock and Kidlington, worked by Train Staff and only one Engine in steam at a time, or two coupled together. No Block Telegraph on this Line. Form of Staff, Round; Colour, Red

Down Trains.

Dis-tance. M.	C.	STATIONS.		Ruling Gra-dient 1 in	B Oxford Auto.	—	B Auto Mixed	—	B Auto.	K Freight RR SX	—	B Auto. ‡	B Auto K SO	B Oxford Auto.	—	B Auto.	—	G Engine and Van. K	B Auto. MSX	B Auto. SO	B Auto. MO	B Auto. N	B Auto. V SO
					a.m.		a.m.		a.m.	noon.		p.m.	p.m.	p.m.		p.m.		p.m.	p.m.	p.m.	p.m.	p.m.	p.m.
—	—	Kidlington	dep.	—	7 23	....	8 40	....	11 15	*12 0*	....	12 38	*1 10*	3 0	....	4 10	....	5† 5	5 38	*5 48*	*5 53*	6 48	*6 54*
2	9	Shipton-on-Cherwell Halt	,,	69 R	7 29	..	8 48	..	11 21	—	..	12 44	*1 16*	3 6	..	4 16	..	—	5 44	*5 54*	*5 59*	6 54	*7 0*
3	57	Blenheim & Woodstock	arr.	129 R	7 33	....	8 53	....	11 25	*12 10*	....	12 48	*1 20*	3 10	....	4 20	....	5†13	5 48	*5 58*	*6 3*	6 58	*7 4*

Up Trains.

STATIONS.		Ruling Gra-dient 1 in	B Auto Mixed.	—	B Auto.	—	G Engine and Van. RR SX	B Auto.	—	B Oxford Auto.	B Auto. K SO	B Oxford Auto. K SO	B Auto.	—	K Freight K	—	B Auto.	—	B Auto.	—	B Auto.	—
			a.m.		a.m.		a.m.	p.m.		p.m.	p.m.	p.m.	p.m.		p.m.		p.m.		p.m.		p.m.	
Blenheim & Woodstock	dep.	—	7 58	....	9 30	....	*11†30*	12 22	....	12 58	*12 58*	*1 25*	3 48	....	4 40	....	5 22	....	6 20	....	7 10	....
Shipton-on-Cherwell Halt	,,	129 F	8 4	..	9 35	..	—	12 27	..	1 3	*1 3*	*1 30*	3 53	..	—	..	5 27	..	6 25	..	7 15	..
Kidlington	arr.	69 F	8 11	....	9 40	....	*11†38*	12 32	....	1 8	*1 8*	*1 35*	3 58	....	4 50	....	5 32	....	6 30	....	7¶20	....

K—Suspended. N—On Saturdays commencing 23rd May, 1953, will start at 6.54 p.m. V—Commences 23rd May, 1953. ‡—May run as a Mixed trip when necessary at point-to-point times shewn for other Mixed trips. ¶—Thence empty to Oxford at 7†25 p.m.

The September 1952 working timetable.

such as those to Abingdon or Morris Cowley, thereby providing a useful 'Cross town' link with consequent savings in fuel and manpower. This would have given Woodstock (and indeed Kidlington) residents a regular through service to Oxford, and might in turn have enabled BR to compete with local bus services — at least for a few more years. Against this, Woodstock was a small town with a population of only 1,600 and it must be admitted that such a small number of people barely justified a train service of any description.

In retrospect the late 1940s and early 1950s were years of complete stagnation in which no attempt was made to run the Blenheim & Woodstock branch economically. Yet few could envisage a time when 'Rosie' would no longer run to Woodstock; railways were still seen as essential public services, and most people assumed that they would be maintained in perpetuity. The news of a possible closure, when announced in June 1951, therefore came as something of a shock, and the *Oxford Mail* predicted 'considerable opposition' from farmers and other people in the district. Meanwhile, BR continued to provide a full train service which was, in its essentials, merely a continuation of the pre-war Great Western timetable. By 1952 there were still eight trains each way including one up and two down through workings, but ominously, when a former engine driver applied for renewal of his travel concession ticket between Kidlington and Woodstock, he was told that the branch had already closed!

Although few local people now made use of their railway, they objected most strongly when they learned that it was to be axed, and several ideas for retention were put forward, notably by Mr O.H. Prosser of the Railway Development Association, who argued that the line could be taken over by a private company. Twenty years later, this might have been a good idea, for the Woodstock branch was entirely self-contained and could have become a profitable steam-worked tourist railway. However, the great days of railway preservation had not yet arrived, and back in 1953 people envisaged a cheaply-run 'light railway'.

Local papers such as the *Oxford Mail* were intrigued by Mr Prosser's suggestion that converted petrol buses might be used, and the *Mail* published a photograph of an ex-Great Northern Railway (Ireland) vehicle in service on the Sligo, Leitrim & Northern Counties line. The *Reading Standard* recalled Lord Cawdor's pioneer rail and road car services in the early 1900s, but omitted to mention that the auto-trains used on the Woodstock branch were in fact the lineal descendants of such vehicles. Supporters of the railbus idea seemed unaware of the vast difference between running a short dead-end spur such as the Woodstock line and a 43¼ mile cross-country route such as the SL & NCR. The remote, under-populated counties of Leitrim and Fermanagh enjoyed few public transport facilities, and in such circumstances the sparse services of the SL & NCR provided a vital lifeline; Woodstock, on the other hand, was well-served by bus services and would, even after closure of its own line, have conveniently situated railheads at Kidlington and Handborough. On a long cross-country route there was no disadvantage in having a single-ended railbus which could be turned at the end of each journey, but such vehicles could hardly be turned after each ten minute trip between Woodstock and Kidlington — in any case there were no turntables!

The railbus idea was clearly something of a red herring, and arguments for and against closure really centred on the provision of alternative public transport services. Mr L.G. Jupp, Works Manager of the Shipton Cement Works, pointed out that many cement workers lived at Bunkers Hill and had no other transport than the railway. Others argued that as over 300 new houses were shortly to be built at Woodstock the railway might shortly have some new customers. One curious suggestion concerned Shipton-on-Cherwell Halt which (ran the argument) was 'too far from the village' and should therefore be resited about half a mile up the line — however, this would have moved it away from Bunkers Hill and the cement workers' families who formed the only body of regular travellers!

The case for closure really rested on ticket sales, which (claimed BR) had declined from approximately 20,000 a year in the 1930s to only 9,000 in 1952. On average, each train carried only 5–6 passengers, and some services were running empty. There was, sadly, no case for retention and the outcome of a meeting held in Oxford by the Transport Users'

A panoramic view of Kidlington station, with the Woodstock auto-train in the branch bay and the goods yard to the right. There was no means of taking water at Kidlington but engines usually filled up at Oxford before the first down trip, and again during the midday crew change, and topped up at Woodstock at intervals throughout the day. When mixed trains arrived at Kidlington, they entered the bay and, after passengers had disembarked, reversed back onto the branch (beyond the bridge) where wagons were left while the loco and trailer ran round onto the other end. The wagons were then placed in the yard and any shunting required, including servicing the bacon factory, was carried out with the trailer still attached. The bacon factory was situated behind the goods shed and served by a siding which crossed the station approach road. *W. A. Camwell*

The last Oxford to Woodstock down train pauses in the up main platform at Oxford, with 'cheerio', 'dear old pal', 'RIP' and other slogans scrawled over the engine. *R. C. Riley*

Consultative Committee was that the Blenheim & Woodstock branch would be closed to all traffic on and from Monday, 1st March 1954, with the last trains running on Saturday, 27th February.

Branch line closures were not new, and as far back as the 1930s the 'Big Four' companies had carried out extensive closure programmes (90 lines were closed in 1930/31 alone). However, there had then been a pause, and when in the early 1950s British Railway embarked on another pruning operation, there was still an air of novelty about each closure, heightened by a feeling that the newly-nationalised railways had become pawns of the government. This was certainly the feeling of Oxford undergraduates who, on the morning of Saturday, 27th February, chalked 'Killed by Govt.', 'cheerio' and other comments on the sides of No 1420.

The Last Train

The line carried many extra travellers on its last day, and photographers could be seen roaming in fields beside the railway, recording the last hours for posterity. No 1420 made her customary return trips to and from Kidlington, hauling trailer No W183W. Although the day was cold, a weak sun cast long shadows across wintry fields which would soon be bursting forth with new life, but, sadly, 'Rosie' would not live to see another spring. At 12.55 pm the branch train ran through to Oxford, arriving as usual in the main up platform, and then crossing to the down bay. In view of the large number of additional travellers, an extra coach was attached to the front of the engine, which was thereby 'sandwiched' between two auto-trailers.

The last through working from Oxford to Blenheim & Woodstock was driven by Harry Collins and fired by Jack Loveridge; the guard, on this final afternoon, was Cecil Watkins. Bill Pomeroy junior had asked if his father, who worked on the line from 1906 until retirement in 1939, could drive the very last departure from Woodstock, but he had been retired for so long that BR would not give the necesary permission, though they agreed that he could ride on the footplate as an honoured guest. Meanwhile, as darkness descended, crowds were gathering at Woodstock and 150 tickets were sold before the last train pulled out to a barrage of exploding detonators and flash bulbs; many people

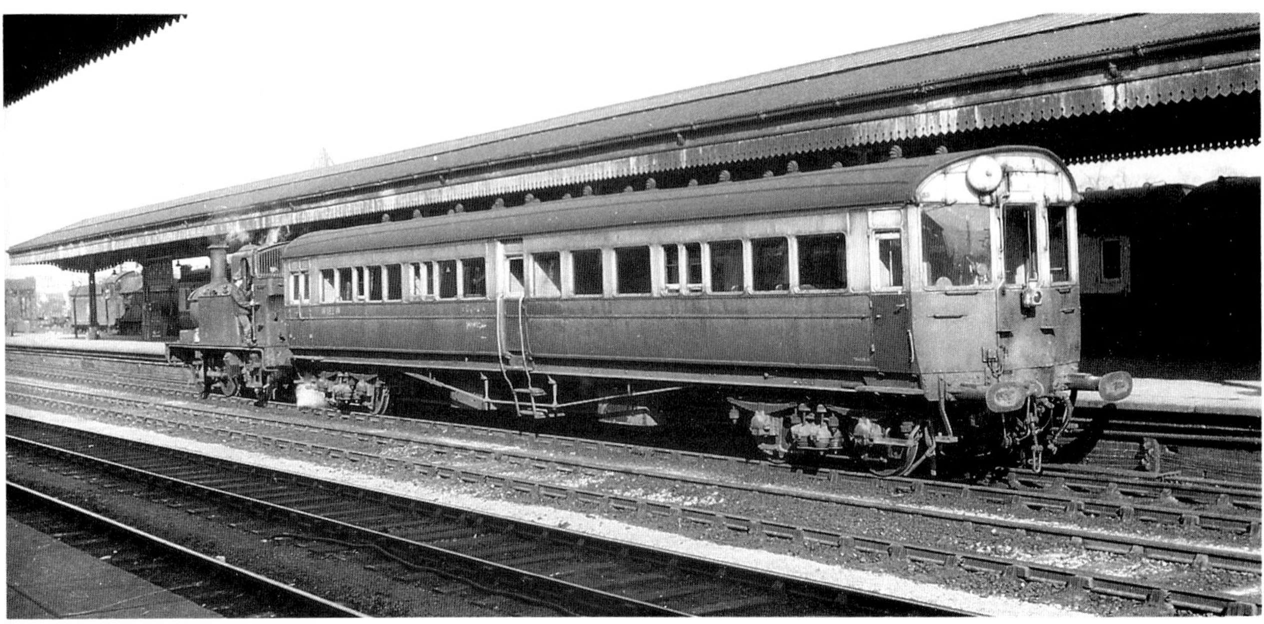

Another view of the branch auto-train at Oxford on its last day. *Dr. G. D. Parkes*

A second auto-car was attached to the Woodstock end of the train during the final afternoon. Here No. 1420 rounds the curve at Shipton-on-Cherwell. Former staff cannot recollect such a train formation on any previous occasion. *R. J. Buckley*

Another view of Shipton-on-Cherwell Halt on the last day of operation. When first opened in 1929, the platform here was of sub-standard height, but in 1933 the entire structure was raised, leaving part of the original platform *in situ* at rail level.
W. A. Camwell

Two views of the last train waiting at Blenheim & Woodstock.
W. A. Camwell & R. C. Riley

watched its departure, while others had gathered by the lineside as the brightly-lit train travelled past darkened fields and woods.

To those on the train, this was a time for memories — of the early years when Lord Randolph, his son Winston Churchill and other celebrities had been regular travellers, of journeys to Oxford on the 'Woolworth Express' and of sheepskins and other commodities arriving daily by train. Above all, people recalled ordinary journeys for work or pleasure, the familiar sight of 'Rosie' with her auto-coach and the sound of steam whistles echoing across the countryside — sights and sounds which would soon become part of history for Woodstock people.

A further barrage of detonators greeted the last train as it reached Shipton-on-Cherwell Halt, and large crowds waited to see the final arrival and departure from Kidlington. The Oxford University Railway Society were out in force, and had placed a wreath on the leading auto-coach. Meanwhile, a small group of photographers had gathered at Oxford, where the last train from Blenheim & Woodstock arrived, some two minutes late.

The full realisation that Woodstock had lost its railway did not really dawn until the following weeks, when people noticed the absence of shunting noises, and saw the locked and deserted station; 'Woodstock did not seem the same' recalled Arthur Scarsbrook.

Finale: The Post-Closure Period and the Last Years of Kidlington

The alternative arrangements for Woodstock coal and glove traffic centred not on Kidlington, but on nearby Handborough, which had a larger goods yard and better vehicular access. To cater for this extra traffic Handborough's siding accommodation was increased, and, in view of its new status, this former OW & WR station became known as 'Handborough *for Blenheim*'. In practice it had been the main station for Woodstock and Blenheim for many years, and visiting VIPs tended to use it more and more after the Woodstock branch was sold to the GWR.

On 30th January 1965 the eyes of the world were focussed on Handborough when it was used by Sir Winston Churchill's funeral special. The train, headed by Southern Region 'Battle of Britain' Pacific No 34051 *Winston Churchill*, ran into the up platform by means of a specially laid facing crossover, and the dead statesman was then taken by hearse to Bladon Church, where he was interred near the graves of his father Lord Randolph Churchill, his uncle the Eighth Duke of Marlborough, his mother Jennie and his sister-in-law Consuelo.

Kidlington remained open for both passenger and freight traffic after the closure of Blenheim & Woodstock, with a service of around six trains each way. In June 1962, for example, there were five up and six down workings — many

The end of an era as track is lifted from the abandoned terminus. *C. L. Turner*

of which continued through to Paddington, Wolverhampton or other destinations, providing a useful service for local residents. In general the daily service was maintained by DMUs, but the 5.55 am Banbury to Princes Risborough and the 5.15 pm Morris Cowley to Banbury were loco-hauled formations. A pick-up freight arrived from Hinksey Yard at 03.09 pm and continued its journey to Banbury at 3.19 pm; an up working called *en route* back to Hinksey at 12.28 pm. There was, in addition, an early morning newspaper train in the down direction at 05.24 am.

By the 1960s Kidlington had become a populous, outer suburb of Oxford, but all new housing developments were situated on the southern side of the village, and, faced with a walk of up to two miles to their 'local' station, few people commuted into Oxford by train. Not surprisingly, Kidlington was listed for closure in the notorious Beeching Report, together with Handborough, Heyford, Bletchington and indeed almost *all* remaining stations in Oxfordshire. In the event, a change of government saved Handborough (which became an unstaffed halt) but not Kidlington, which was closed on Monday, 2nd November 1964, the last trains calling on the preceding Saturday. Kidlington's final hours were recorded by *Oxford Mail* reporter Allan Brookes, whose words captured the melancholic atmosphere of a station closure: 'the last passengers have gone. The booking office window has slammed shut for the last time . . . trains speed through and . . . Kidlington . . . is now for the rail traveller just a group of deserted buildings by the lineside, just a name printed in an out-of-date timetable'.

The Woodstock branch had, meanwhile, been lifted, though not immediately and not in its entirety. The line remained *in situ* for over three years and lifting did not take place until 1957; this melancholy task was carried out by Messrs Pittrail and completed by January 1958. Thereafter the terminal buildings at Woodstock were purchased by the owner of Young's Garage and eventually converted into garage buildings.

At Kidlington, the branch remained intact from its bay platform as far as Thrupp, a distance of about 40 chains. The platform line was lifted in 1965, but the rest of the line served as a running loop until 1968; interestingly, BR working timetables continued to refer to this loop as the 'Blenheim Branch' long after the closure of the branch proper! By 1969, however, this last section of the Blenheim & Woodstock branch had been lifted, and with its removal a last tenuous link with the past was broken; the branch was well and truly dead.

Kidlington station was used by a printing firm after its closure, though the up side buildings and platforms were demolished. The steel footbridge which once linked both platforms was later taken down and re-erected near Didcot North Junction, where it replaced a similar bridge that had been badly damaged by blazing tanker wagons after a derailment.

There were, throughout the 1970s, suggestions that Kidlington could be re-opened as a 'Park and Ride' station for local commuters. Roundham Lane Crossing would have been an ideal location for such a facility, being very near the centre of Kidlington; furthermore it had good road access and there was at that time ample room for the necessary car park. British Rail was enthusiastic, but insisted that local councils should 'put their money where their mouth was' and provide financial help. Naturally, such assistance was not forthcoming (from either the County or District Councils) and nearby open land has been 'developed', leaving insufficient room for an approach road and car park should the idea be raised again at some future date. Similar schemes have been put forward for Handborough, where the existing platform and car park already forms a convenient 'Park and Ride' facility for Woodstock. Sadly, although extra train services have been provided on various occasions, local commuters seem to prefer an agonising crawl through Oxford's daily traffic jams to the comfort and speed of rail travel, and it seems that as far as Woodstock people are concerned, the Railway Age is now well and truly finished.

The Railway Today

Most disused railways can still be followed by foot, enabling enthusiasts or local historians to mentally recreate the appearance of these railways as they would have been prior to closure. Sadly, this is not possible in the case of the Woodstock line which, though still visible, has become impassable. Fortunately, the former branch is flanked by public roads and footpaths, which enable its approximate course to be followed.

Kidlington station building can still be seen beside the busy Oxford to Birmingham main line. Regrettably, the distinctive Brunelian goods shed was demolished in 1984, and much of the surrounding area is now occupied by an industrial estate. The former Woodstock branch alignment has been obscured by deep ballasting on the adjacent main line, but its course can still be identified; a good access point is the public footpath from Shipton-on-Cherwell Church to Hampton Gay, which crosses the line near Hampton Gay Church. From here, walkers can reach Thrupp Curve by returning to the canal towpath and crossing the waterway by means of an Oxford Canal 'drawbridge' to the east of the railway.

The Woodstock branch girder bridge has been dismantled, but its solid red brick abutments can still be seen, and walkers who cross the canal via the above-mentioned lift bridge can (with difficulty) scale the branch embankment, or else continue to Shipton village along a public footpath. Those attempting to follow the railway will rapidly come to jungle-like vegetation and an area of old prams, abandoned cars and accumulated detritus.

Proceeding westwards, the cutting behind Shipton village has been filled with domestic refuse and grassed-over. Farm buildings now occupy part of the alignment, but walkers can make use of the cement company's private road, which remains a public right-of-way. To the left the railway's great, curving embankment still dominates the surrounding landscape like some historic defensive feature. Saplings have, in the years since closure, grown into sturdy trees, and any potential 'paths' along the old embankment are blocked by hawthorn and blackberry bushes. It is impossible to penetrate more than a few yards, even in winter when the undergrowth is much thinner. The Cement Works road follows the railway for half a mile, with good views of Shipton quarry to the right; sadly, dumper trucks have replaced the former quarry railway, though a small diesel engine has been retained for use in the surviving exchange sidings.

At Shipton-on-Cherwell Halt, the Banbury Road bridge has been taken down and the halt itself has left no traces, other than the broken 'kissing gate' at the bottom of the embankment. The site of the halt is covered in thick undergrowth and access to the track bed is virtually impossible, but those wishing to reach Woodstock can do so by following the A423 for a short distance and then turning right along the A4095. Another right turn leads to a minor road which runs parallel to the railway for a short distance before turning sharp right and passing beneath it to reach Shipton Slade Farm; the overbridge here has been dismantled and, although it is possible to climb the embankments on each side, the track bed is obstructed by bushes and trees. It is necessary, therefore, to continue towards Woodstock along a bridleway which runs parallel to the railway on its south side (alternatively, there is a public footpath running westwards from Slade Farm).

The deep cutting between Woodstock and Shipton has been filled with refuse and sown with grass seed (thereby obliterating an entire section of the line) but the route becomes visible on the outskirts of Woodstock, where a section of embankment remains. The station site has now been completely 'redeveloped' and the goods yard, coal wharves, cattle dock and passenger platform have been replaced by roads, houses and a telephone exchange. Only the terminal buildings remain, with large plate-glass windows inserted into the Oxford Road façade and various additions and extensions at the rear. Although the front of the building is quite smart, the former platform area is littered with wrecked cars, diesel storage tanks, and all the clutter of a busy garage business.

In addition to the major earthworks, diligent railway archaeologists may find smaller items of interest along the route, notably a variety of old rails, used as fences, notice supports or on surrounding farms. There are three main types, including conventional bullhead rail of differing sizes, former broad gauge bridge rails, and — perhaps most interestingly — an unusual type of light flat-bottomed rail. This may be a relic of Lucas & Aird's contractors railway, or (more likely) it may have originated in the nearby Shipton Cement Works.

Finally, it would be appropriate to mention that no less than three of the line's regular locomotives have been preserved, and in a sense these constitute 'Rosie's' most tangible memorial. Nos 1420 and 1450 are on the Dart Valley Railway in Devon, while sister engine No 1442 is a static exhibit at Tiverton.

Appendix 1 – SOME PERSONALITIES

George, Fourth Duke of Marlborough (1739–1818): A major supporter of the Oxford Canal, which was opened throughout to Oxford in 1790; in 1789 he opened a connecting waterway from the canal to the River Thames at Wolvercote, and in 1800 the Duke initiated a scheme for improvement of the River Evenlode at Cassington. These activities can be seen as forerunners of the later railway scheme.

Isambard Kingdom Brunel (1806–1859): Engineer of the GWR and most of its early subsidiaries, including the Oxford Worcester & Wolverhampton Railway and the Oxford & Rugby line; as such he probably designed Woodstock Road station, which later (as 'Kidlington') became the junction for Woodstock.

John Winston Spencer Churchill, Seventh Duke of Marlborough (1822–1883): The first Churchill to become involved with railways when the Oxford Worcester & Wolverhampton and Oxford & Rugby lines were built across his land. Married the eldest daughter of the Third Marquis of Londonderry; father of the Eighth and Ninth Dukes, and of Lord Randolph Churchill. Served as Tory MP for Woodstock from 1840–45 and again from 1847 until 1857; Viceroy of Ireland 1876–80, and on his return to Woodstock suggested a scheme whereby land would be provided, free of charge, to the GWR if the latter were to build a branch line from Woodstock Road station.

George Charles Spencer Churchill, Eighth Duke of Marlborough (1844–1892): Eldest son of the Seventh Duke, whom he succeeded in 1883. Married Albertha, daughter of the First Duke of Abercorn in 1869, but divorced her in 1883 and later married Lilly Hammersley of New York. The founder of the Woodstock Railway and its Chairman until his death in 1893. An irresolute individual, the Eighth Duke is unlikely to have launched the Woodstock Railway entirely on his own initiative, and it is possible that Lord Randolph Churchill (q.v. below) provided the initial impetus for a scheme that had first been suggested by the Seventh Duke.

Lord Randolph Churchill (1849–1925): The third son of John Winston, and brother of the railway-building Eighth Duke. A brilliant, but enigmatic figure, who may have persuaded his brother to build the railway so that Blenheim Palace could be used as the setting for political rallies. Originally MP for Woodstock, he became the Member for Paddington South when his local borough was disfranchised in 1885. Having evolved his own brand of 'Tory Democracy' (the so-called 'Fourth Party'), he rose to high office, becoming Chancellor of the Exchequer and Leader of the House of Commons, but his erratic behaviour and quick temper made many enemies and he effectively destroyed his own career. Insofar as his political beliefs can be summarised, he was a democrat who nevertheless viewed his own class as 'natural' leaders of a politically-aware working class electorate; his views on the position of Ireland within the United Kingdom were particularly strong (perhaps because of his Irish mother). Lord Randolph married an American heiress, Miss Jeannette Jerome, and their first child was Winston Spencer Churchill, the future Prime Minister. Served as Tory MP for Paddington South from 1885 until 1895.

Sir John Aird: Son of John Aird, a Scottish crofter who founded a major contracting business, specialising in railways, dams and harbour works (often in conjunction with C.T. Lucas, though the two firms also functioned independently). Knighted in 1901, John Aird was Tory MP for North Paddington from 1887 until 1905, and also its first Mayor. Although the Woodstock branch was built by Lucas & Aird in partnership, John Aird seems to have been the dominant figure, attending Board meetings and influencing company policy. In the absence of any positive leadership on the part of the Eighth Duke, John Aird inevitably became a leading figure in the Woodstock Railway Company, and, apart from the initial problem over Woodstock Road, the contractor handled the company's affairs in a capable and businesslike manner until its eventual sale to the GWR. It would probably be true to say that John Aird was the Woodstock Railway's most capable supporter.

Charles Lucas (1820–1895): A partner in the firm of Lucas Brothers, and, with John Aird, one half of the Lucas & Aird partnership. Charles Lucas became a director of the Woodstock Railway Company in July 1890, but was less active than John Aird; his main contribution came in 1893 when he attempted to sell the company to the GWR.

Charles Richard John Spencer Churchill, Ninth Duke of Marlborough (1871–1934): Succeeded his father the Eighth Duke in 1892, and became a director of the Woodstock Railway Company in February 1893. The Ninth Duke displayed little interest in the railway and the first attempts to sell it to the GWR were made soon after he became Duke. Served in South Africa with the Imperial Yeomanry, and later held various minor Government posts.

Consuelo, Ninth Duchess of Marlborough: Like his brothers, the Ninth Duke married an extremely rich American heiress, bringing her to Woodstock by train on 31st March 1896; *Fair Rosamund* may have been named for this occasion. Perhaps because her character and appearance did not really suit polite society, the new Duchess of Marlborough spent much of her time at Blenheim and is still remembered with affection (she would for example personally thank station staff for holding doors open and similar courtesies).

Appendix 2 – LOCOMOTIVES ALLOCATED TO WOODSTOCK SHED

Year	*Number*	*Class*
1902	549	'517' 0-4-2T
1903	221	” ”
1904	221	” ”
1905	221*	” ”
	1473	” ”
1906	546	” ”
	1473	” ”
1907	218	” ”
	534	” ”
	1473	” ”
1908	203	” ”
	522	” ”
	1289	'1076' 0-6-0ST
	1473	'517' 0-4-2T
1909	1472	” ”
1910	522	” ”
	549	” ”
	1472	” ”
1911	220	” ”
	1423	” ”
	1472	” ”
	1473	” ”
1912	1472	” ”
1913	220	” ”
	522	” ”
	1423	” ”
	1473	” ”
1914	220*	” ”
	522	” ”
1915	220	” ”
	522	” ”
	1427	” ”
	1473	” ”
1916	1438	” ”
	1473	” ”
1917	1438	” ”
	1473	” ”
1918	519	” ”
	588	'481' 2-4-0
	1438	'517' 0-4-2T
	1473	” ”
1919	203	” ”
	1473	” ”
1920	–	–
1921	541	'517' 0-4-2T
	1473	” ”
1922	1443	” ”
	1473	” ”
1923	541	” ”
	1473	” ”
1924	541	” ”
	1473	” ”
1925	1473	” ”
	1484	” ”
1926	1484	” ”

**Shown as Woodstock based but not officially listed as shedded there during the year. However, it should be borne in mind that other locos beside those listed would have stood in during washouts, etc.*

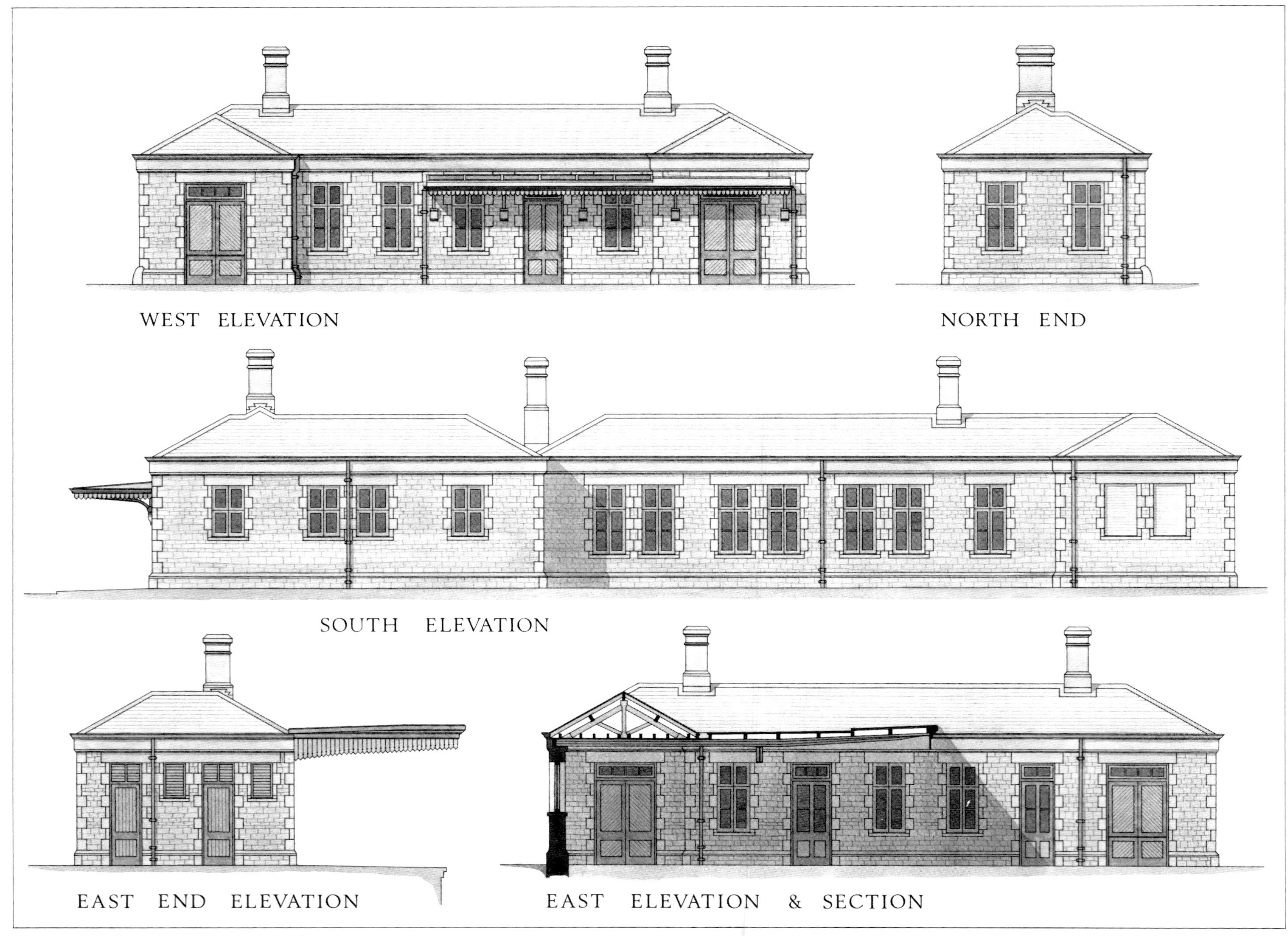
WEST ELEVATION
NORTH END
SOUTH ELEVATION
EAST END ELEVATION
EAST ELEVATION & SECTION

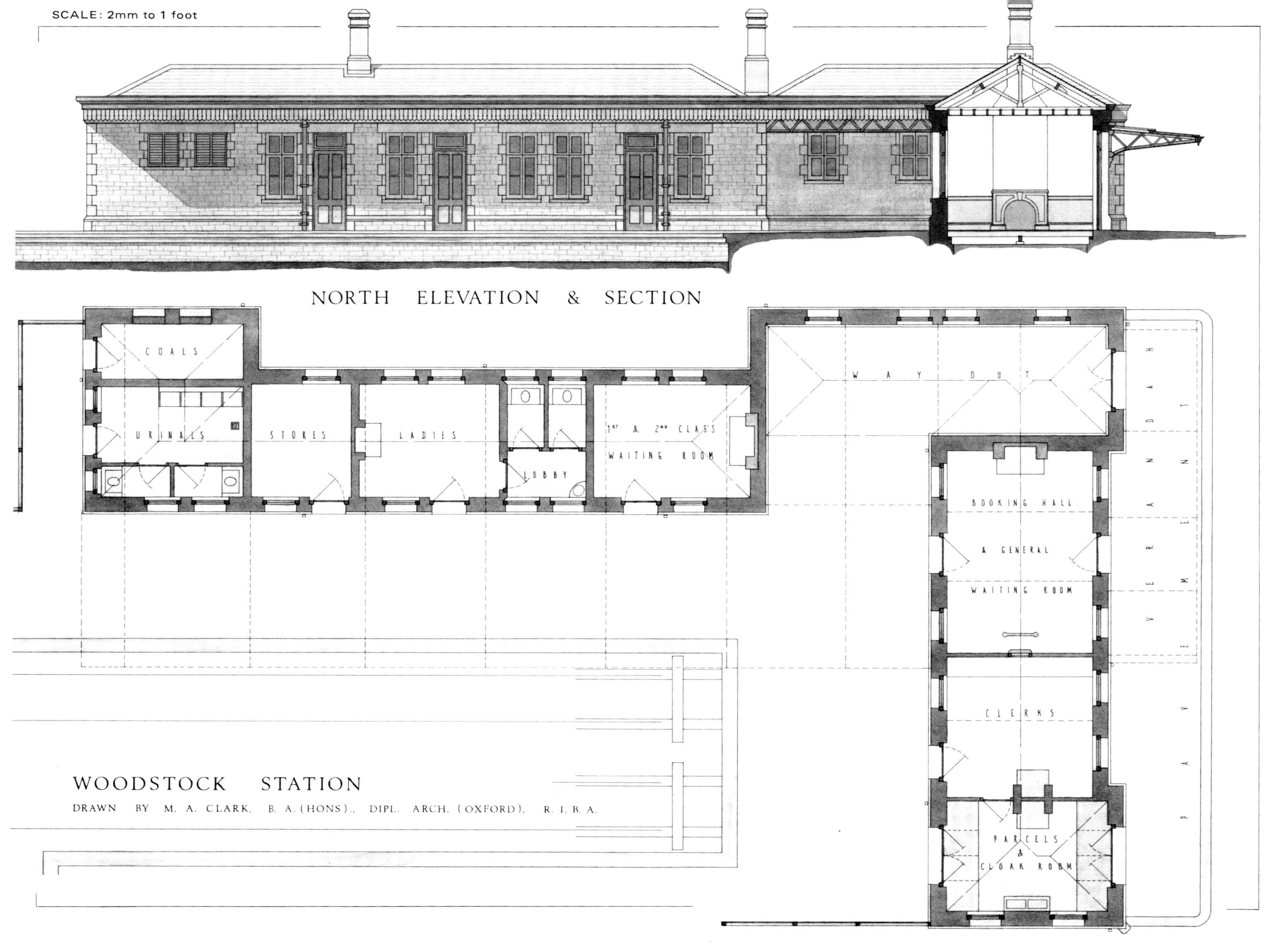
SCALE: 2mm to 1 foot
NORTH ELEVATION & SECTION
COALS
URINALS
STORES
LADIES
LOBBY
1ST & 2ND CLASS WAITING ROOM
WAY OUT
BOOKING HALL & GENERAL WAITING ROOM
CLERKS
PARCELS & CLOAK ROOM
PAVEMENT
VERANDAH
WOODSTOCK STATION
DRAWN BY M. A. CLARK, B. A. (HONS)., DIPL. ARCH. (OXFORD), R. I. B. A.

WOODSTOCK GOODS SHED

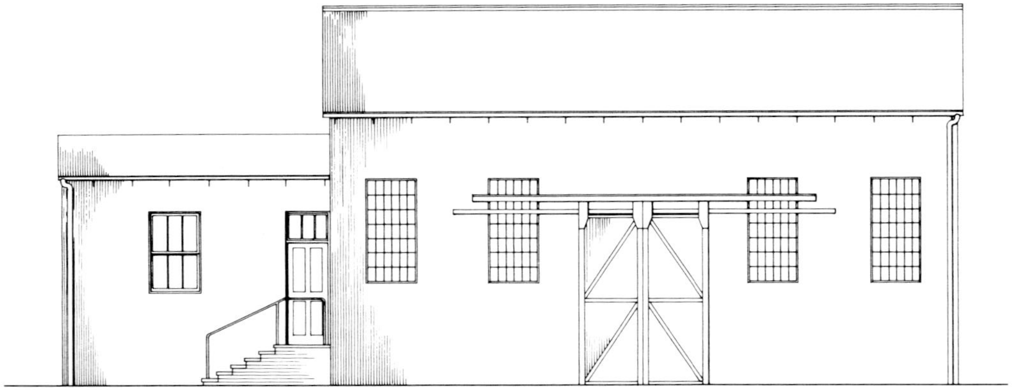

FORECOURT ELEVATION

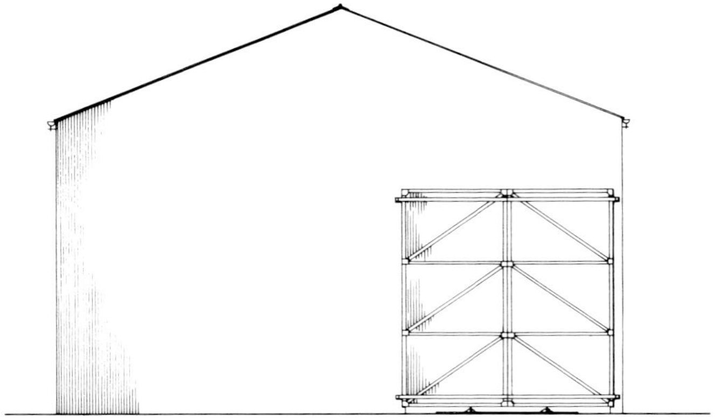

WEST END ELEVATION

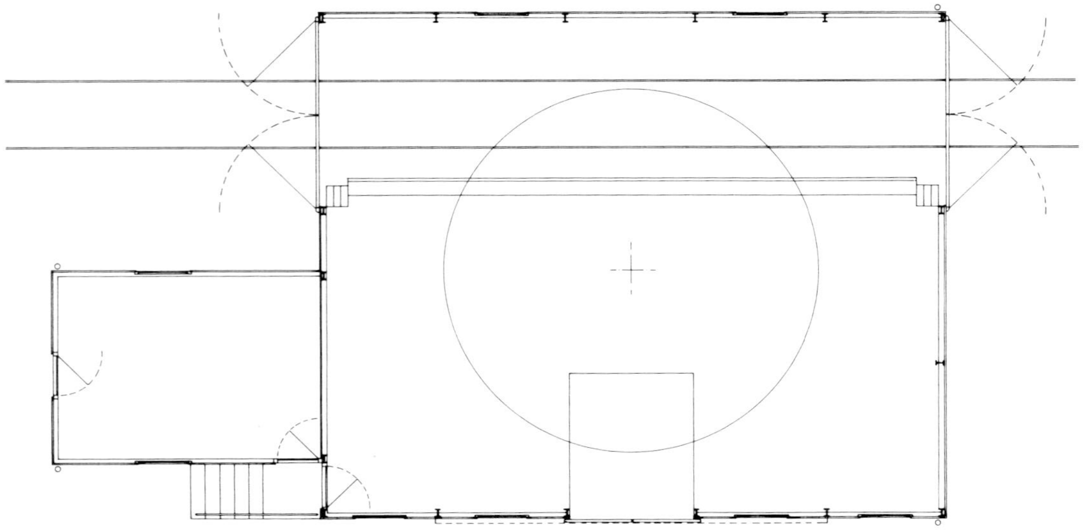

PLAN

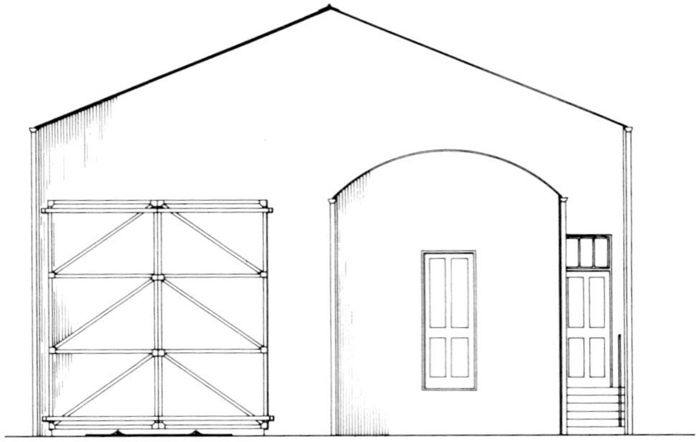

EAST END ELEVATION

SCALE: 2mm to 1 foot

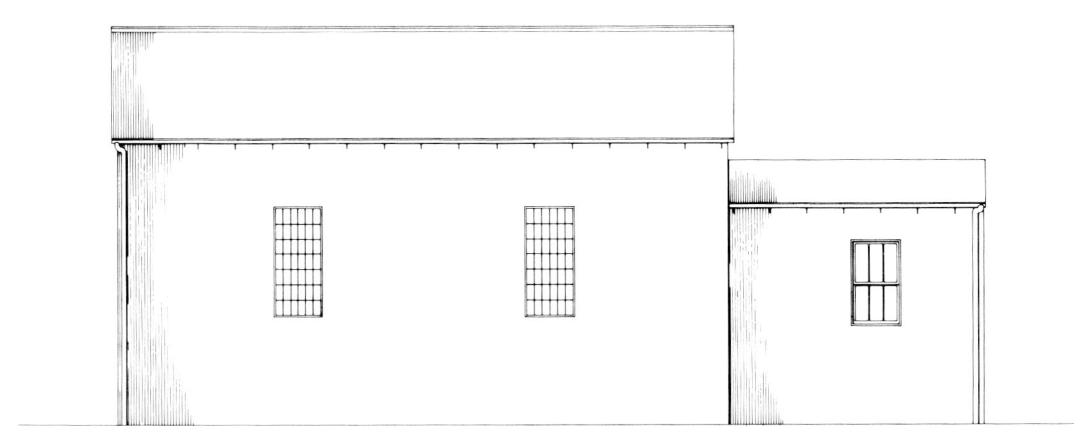

SOUTH ELEVATION

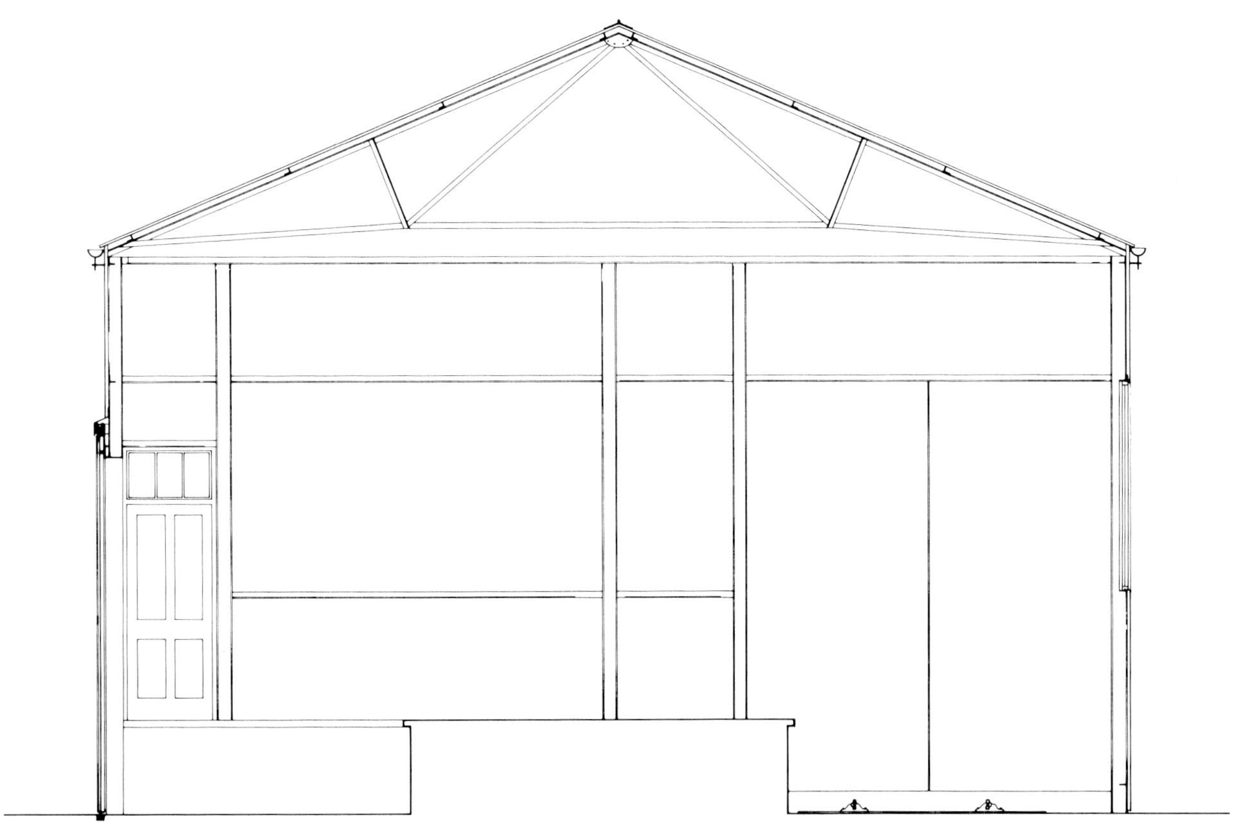

CROSS SECTION

CROSS SECTION 4mm to 1 foot

WOODSTOCK ENGINE SHED

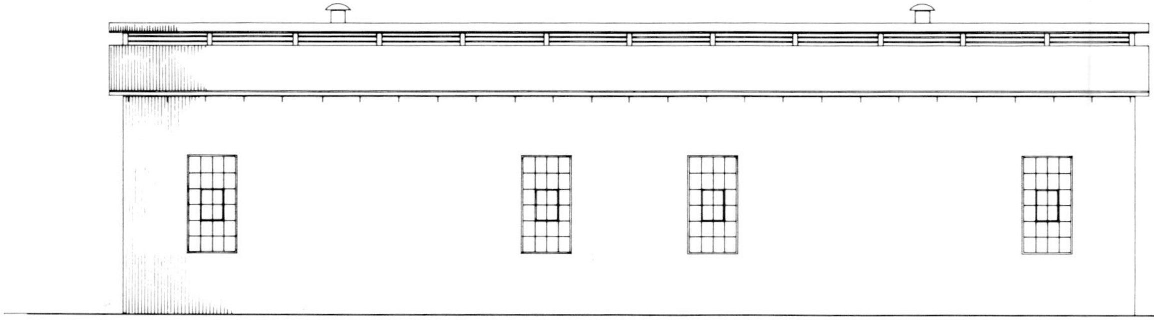

SIDE ELEVATION

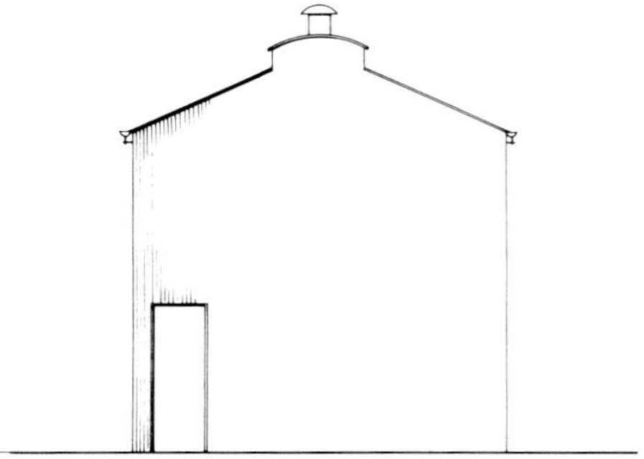

REAR ELEVATION

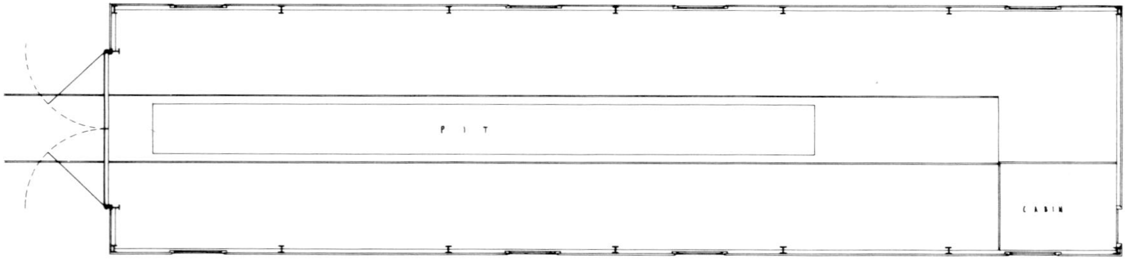

PIT

CABIN

PLAN

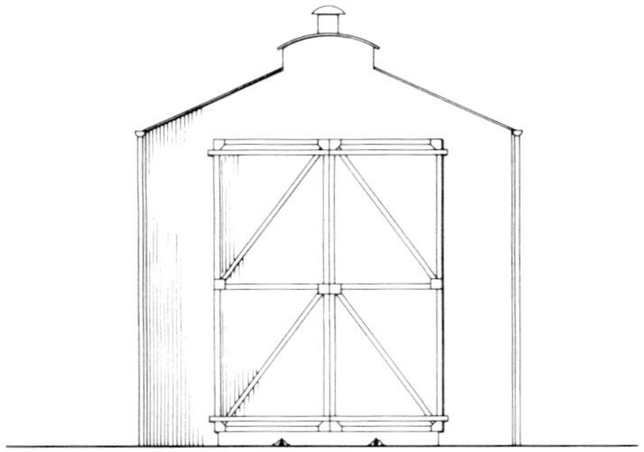

FRONT ELEVATION

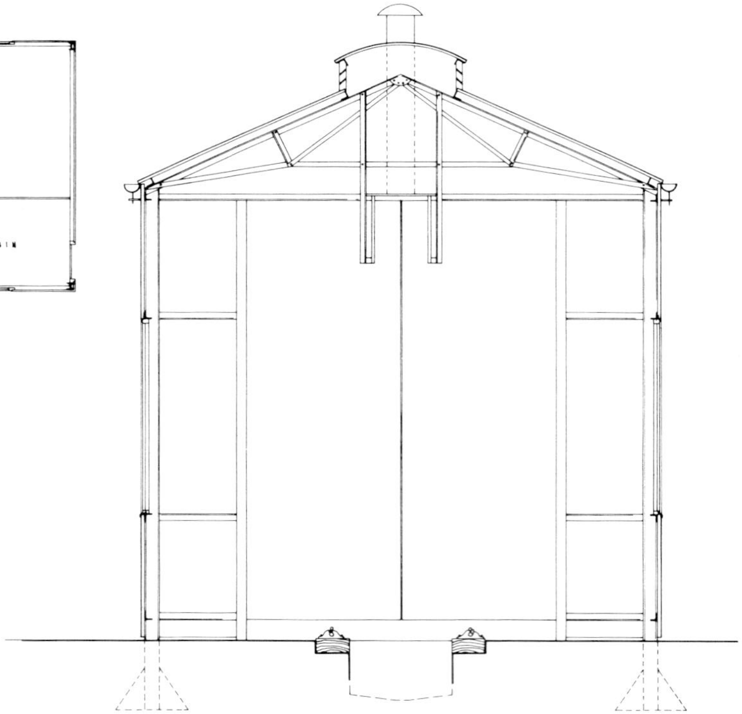

CROSS SECTION

SCALE: 2mm to 1 foot   Cross Section 4mm to 1 foot

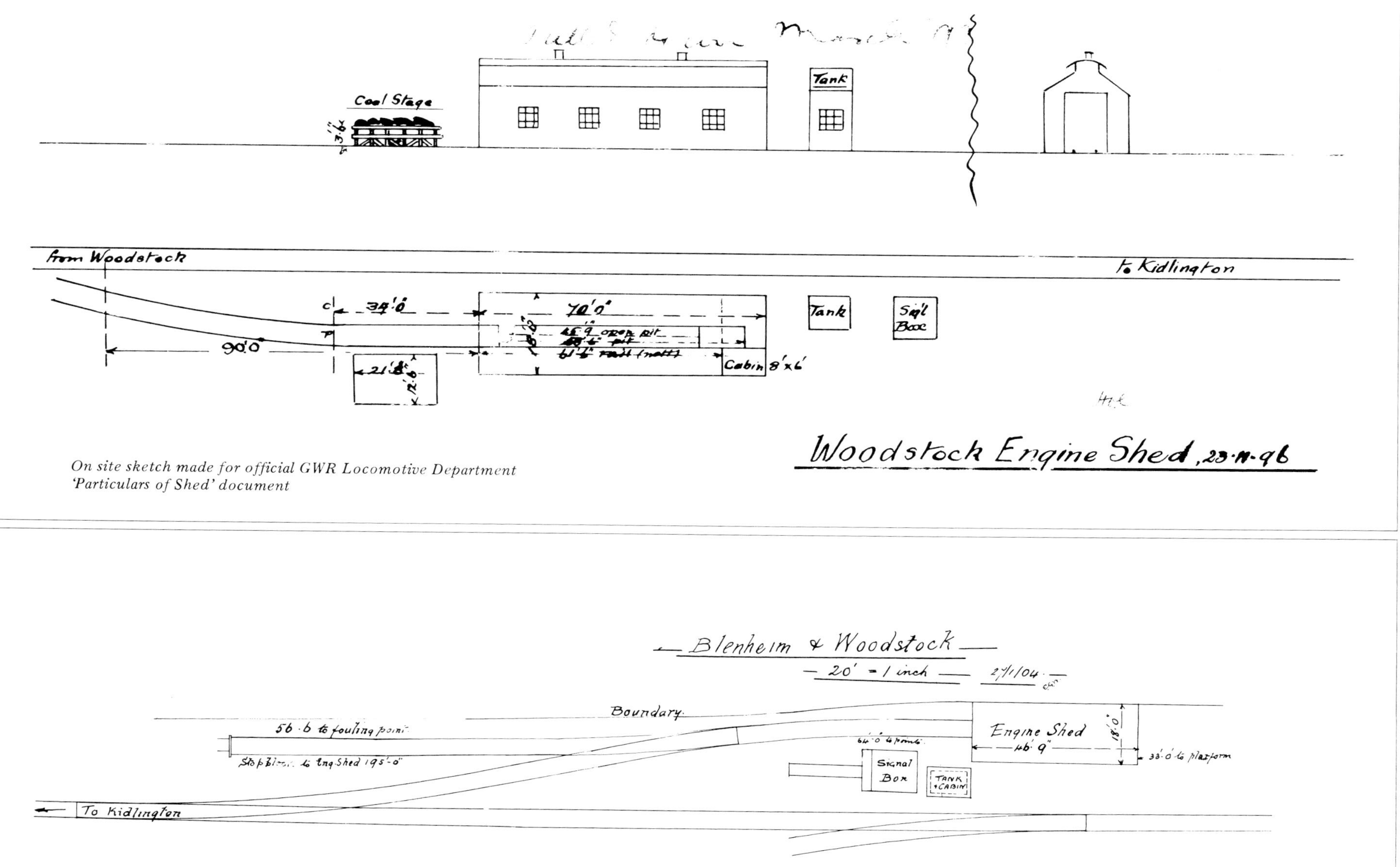

On site sketch made for official GWR Locomotive Department 'Particulars of Shed' document

Taken from later Locomotive Department plan showing restoration of the engine shed after the 1899 agricultural show, with shortened building on the new siding. As the coaling stage was not replaced, it seems likely that coal was replenished at Oxford shed, but a standby coal wagon could well have been stabled on the short siding.

WOODSTOCK WATER TOWER

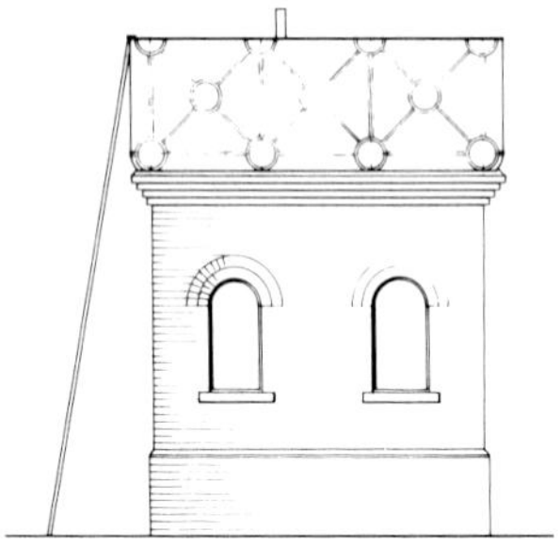

SOUTH ELEVATION

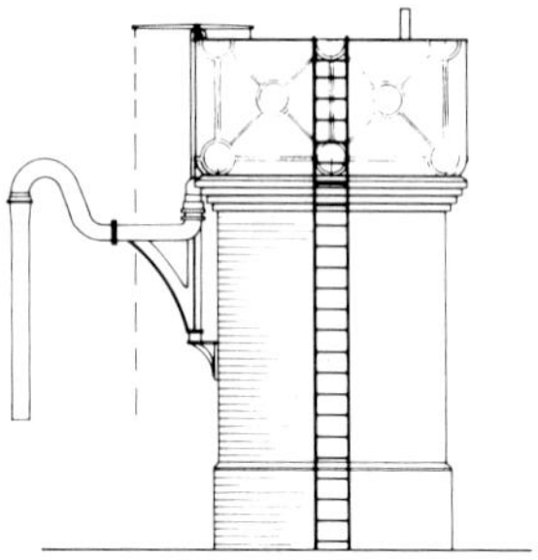

WEST ELEVATION

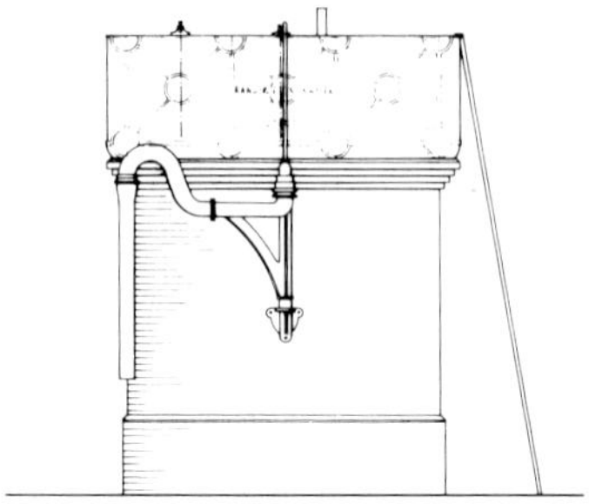

NORTH ELEVATION

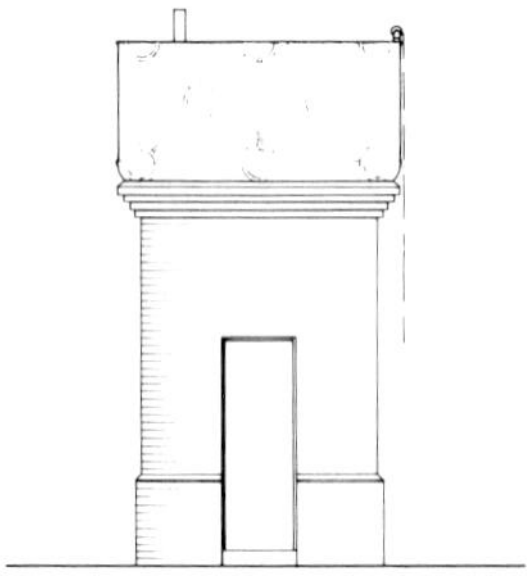

EAST ELEVATION

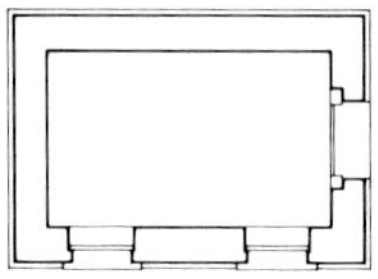

PLAN

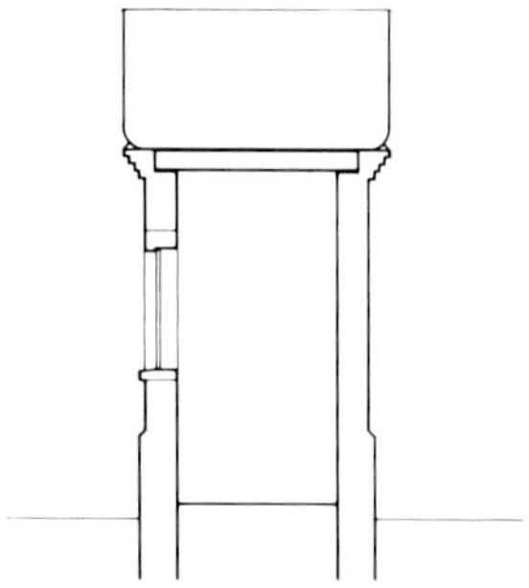

CROSS SECTION

Water Crane as originally proposed

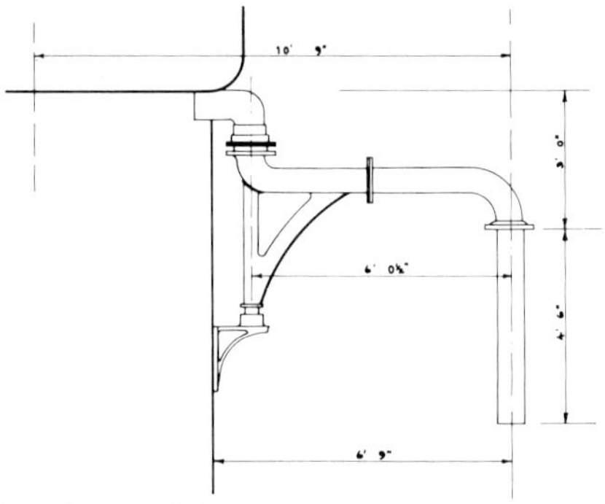

SCALE: 4mm to 1 foot

SCALE: 2mm to 1 foot

WOODSTOCK WEIGH HOUSE

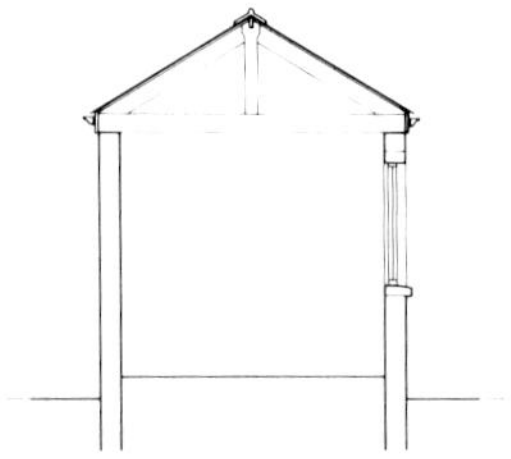

CROSS SECTION

NORTH ELEVATION

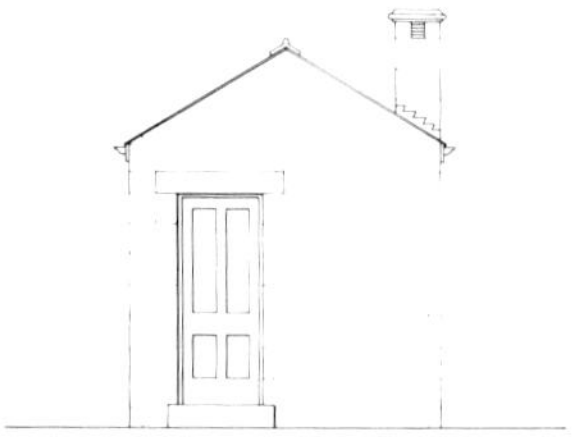

WEST ELEVATION

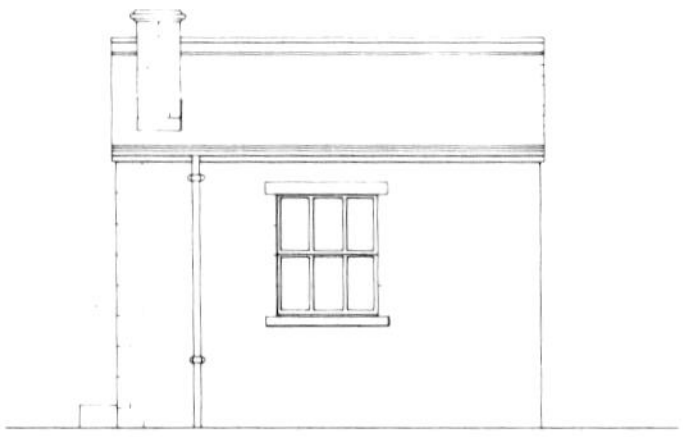

SOUTH ELEVATION

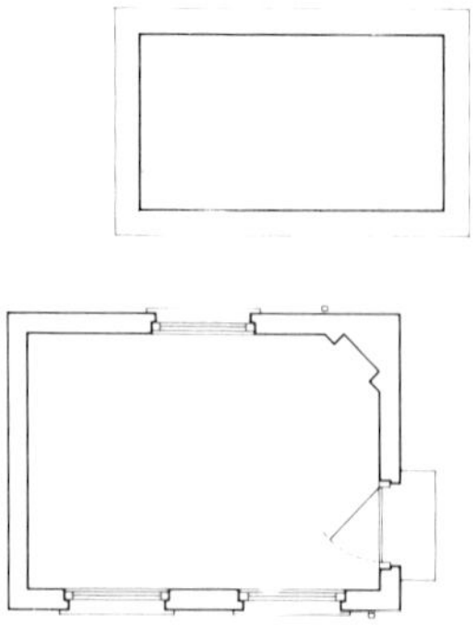

PLAN

SCALE: 2mm to 1 foot